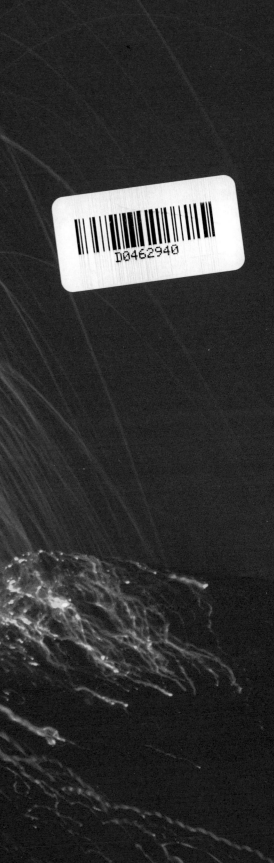

EXPLORING SCIENCE

VOLCANOES & EARTHQUAKES

AN AMAZING FACT FILE AND HANDS-ON PROJECT BOOK

With 19 easy-to-do experiments and 280 exciting pictures

ROBIN KERROD
CONSULTANT: JOHN FARNDON

ARMADILLO

This edition is published by Armadillo, an imprint of Anness Publishing Ltd, 108 Great Russell Street, London WC1B 3NA; info@anness.com

www.annesspublishing.com

If you like the images in this book and would like to investigate using them for publishing, promotions or advertising, please visit our website www.practicalpictures.com for more information.

© Anness Publishing Ltd 2013

Publisher: Joanna Lorenz
Editors: Peter Harrison, Elizabeth Young
Additional material: Steve Parker
Special photography: John Freeman
Stylist: Melanie Williams
Designer: Caroline Grimshaw
Picture Researcher: Kay Rowley
Illustrator: Peter Bull Art Studio
Production Controller: Pirong Wang

The publishers would like to thank the following children, and their parents, for appearing in this book – Anum Butt, Dima Degtyarov, Roxanne Game, Fawwaz Ghany, Angelica Hambrier, Larrissa Henderson, Lori Hey, Louis Loucaides, Malak Mroue, Tom Swaine-Jameson, Sophie Viner.

PICTURE CREDITS
b=bottom, t=top, c= central, l= left, r= right
Bryan & Cherry Alexander: page 48bl. Ardea/R Gibbons: page 19tl;/F Gohier page 17b;/ A Warren page 37cl. BBC Natural History Unit/B Davidson: page 35br;/C Buxton page 34bl. Biofotos: page 27tr;/B Rogers page 34br;/S Summerhays pages 8tr, 56br. Bridgeman Art Library: page 41tr. CEPHAS/M Rock page 35bl. Bruce Coleman: page 7br;/C Atlantide page 22br;/ F Bruemmer page 35c;/G Cubitt page 15cr;/M Freeman page 60t. Corbis p41bl, 53br, 61t, 61br. FLPA/M Withers: page 27bl;/S Ardito(Panda Photo) page 53tr;/S Jonasson page 11cr;/ S McCutcheon pages 33bl, 49cl. Gamma/Frank Spooner: pages 23cl, 47br, 49t, 60br, 60bl, 61tl, 61bl. Genesis Space Photo Library: page 53tl. GSF Picture Library: page 26tl. Robert Harding Picture Library: page 5cl;/R Frerck(Odyssey;/Chicago) page 49bl. Michael Holford: pages 16tl, 54t. Hulton-Getty: page 4tr. Image Select: page 22bl;/Caltech: page 52b. JS Library: page 56bl;/ G Tonsich page 25cr. Landform Slides: page 29cr. Mountain Camera/J Cleare page 48t;/ T Kajiyama pages 45br, 50t, 51cr. Oxford Scientific Films/J Frazier: page 33tl, 63tl;/V Pared page 5bl;/W Faioley page 53c. Planet Earth/Bourseiller&Durieux: pages 32br, 57t;/C Weston pages 17tr, 28b;/I & V Krafft pages 2, 5tr&br, 23bl, 45cl;/J Corripio page 23cr;/J Waters page 7cl;/ K Lucas pages 33tr, 33br;/R Chesher page 10tr;/R Hessler page 11tl;/R Jureit page 36br;/ WM Smithey page 34tl. Rex Features: pages 1, 22tl, 45bl, 46t. Science Photo Library: pages 5tl, 6tr, 11cl, 11bl, 11br, 14tl, 17tl, 17cl, 18c, 19cl, 40br, 63br;/A Pasieka page 30tl;/D Hardy pages 3tl, 29l, 40tl;/D Parker pages 3tl, 44t, 56t;/D Weintraub page 26c, endpapers;/G Garradd page 41c;/G Olson page 49br;/GECO(UK) page 58t;/J Hinsch page 32b;/JL Charmet page 44b;/ L Cook page 49cr;/NASA pages 42t;/P Menzel page 45t;/R de Guglielmo page 32tr;/S Fraser pages 3tl, 28t, 36t, 36bl, 37cr, 38tr;/S Stammers pages 33c, 42bl;/US Geological Survey pages 3br, 42bl, 43t, 45cr. Spacecharts: pages 3cl, 15cl, 23br, 26bl, 26br, 42br, 43c, 43b, 57bl. Still Pictures;/ A Maslennikov: page 37t;/C Caldicott page 29br;/G&M Moss page 17cr. Telegraph Colour Library: pages 3cr, 20tl. Topham Picture Point: pages 27br, 53bl, 61cr. Tony Waltham: pages 3t, 3bl, 6b, 7bl, 15t, 15br, 18b, 19bl, 23t, 27tl, 35t, 37b, 41tl, 57br. Woodmansterne: page 29tr.

Manufacturer: Anness Publishing Ltd, 108 Great Russell Street, London WC1B 3NA, England
For Product Tracking go to: www.annesspublishing.com/tracking
Batch: 6944-22723-1127

CONTENTS

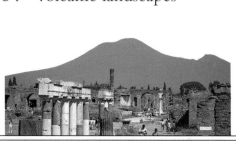

FIRE FROM BELOW

At this moment in various parts of the world volcanoes are erupting. Fountains of red-hot rock are hurtling high into the air and rivers of lava are cascading down the volcanoes' sides. Volcanoes are places where molten (liquid) rock pushes up from below through splits in the Earth's crust. They may be beautiful but they can also be very destructive. Earthquakes are another destructive part of nature. Every year violent earthquakes destroy towns and kill hundreds, sometimes thousands, of people. The constant movements that take place in and beneath the rocky crust that covers the Earth cause volcanoes and earthquakes. The word volcano comes from the name that the people of ancient Rome gave to their god of fire. He was called Vulcan. Volcanology is the term given to the study of volcanoes and the scientists who study them are known as volcanologists.

The greatest
An artist's impression of the massive eruption of the volcano Krakatoa, near Java in south-east Asia, in 1883.

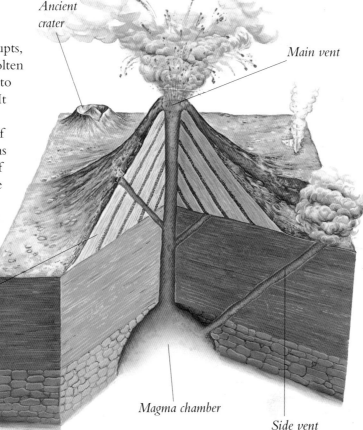

From the depths
When a volcano erupts, magma (red-hot molten rock) forces its way to the Earth's surface. It shoots into the air along with clouds of ash and gas, and runs out over the sides of the volcano. In time layers of ash and lava build up to form a huge cone shape.

Ancient crater

Main vent

Layers of lava and ash

Magma chamber

Side vent

FACT BOX

• The explosion of Krakatoa in Indonesia, in 1883 caused a massive tidal wave that killed 36,000 people.

• In January 1995, a powerful earthquake killed almost 6,500 people in the city of Kobe, Japan. Kobe was one of the country's largest ports and thousands of homes were destroyed. Repairing the damage to the city and surrounding area cost $100 billion.

Piping hot
Hot water often bubbles to the surface in volcanic regions. This creates geothermal (heated in the earth) springs. The hot spring pictured is in Yellowstone National Park in the USA.

Suited up
Heatproof suits and helmets like this make it possible for volcanologists to walk near red-hot lava. This volcanologist is taking samples of lava on the volcano Mauna Loa, on Hawaii.

Out of this world
There are huge volcanoes like this on the planet Venus. Volcanoes have helped shape many bodies in the Solar System, including Mars and the Moon.

Shaking earth
A badly-damaged village in India after a severe earthquake in 1993. Two plates (sections) of the Earth's crust meet in India. The plates push against each other and cause earthquakes.

Red-hot river
A river of molten rock races down the sides of the Hawaiian volcano Kilauea in a 1994 eruption. Kilauea is one of the most active volcanoes known on Earth.

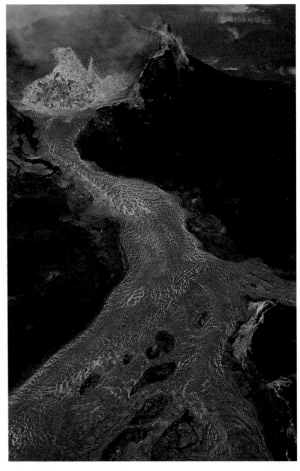

THE ACTIVE EARTH

The causes of volcanoes and earthquakes begin many miles beneath the surface of the Earth. Our planet is covered with a thin layer of hard rock called the crust. Soil, in which trees and plants grow, has built up on top of the rock. Underneath the hard rock of the crust, however, there is a much hotter layer of the Earth called the mantle. The core of the Earth, deep inside the mantle, is intensely hot. That heat moves out from the core and heats everything in the mantle. In the mantle the rocks become semi-liquid and they move and flow like treacle. Because of the intense heat from the core of the Earth, the rocks move in currents. Very hot liquid rocks (magma) are lighter than cooler rocks and float up towards the top of the mantle. Where there are gaps in the crust, the magma bubbles up through them and shoots out in volcanoes.

Volcanoes have been erupting on Earth for billions of years. During all that time they have pushed out enormous amounts of lava (magma pushed out of a volcano), ash and rocks. These hardened and built up in layers to form part of the landscapes around us. Volcanoes also produced water vapour that eventually condensed (turned to liquid) to form the Earth's seas and oceans.

The newborn Earth
Thousands of millions of years ago the Earth probably looked similar to the picture above. Molten rock was erupting from volcanoes everywhere on the Earth's surface, creating huge lava flows. These hardened into rocks.

Fit for giants
Looking like a spectacular, jumbled-up stairway, this rock formation is on the coast of County Antrim in Northern Ireland. It is known as the Giant's Causeway, because people in the past believed that giants built it. However, it is a natural formation made up of six-sided columns of basalt, one of the commonest volcanic rocks. Basalt often forms columns like these when it cools, and this is called columnar basalt. There are similar structures on Staffa, an island in the Inner Hebrides group off north-western Scotland. Among the many caves along Staffa's coastline is Fingal's Cave, about which the composer Mendelssohn wrote a famous overture.

Inside the Earth

The Earth is made up of a number of different layers. The top layer is the hard crust. It is thinnest under the oceans, where it is only some 5–10km/3–6 miles thick. Underneath the crust there is a thick layer of semi-liquid rock known as the mantle. Beneath the mantle is a layer of liquid metal, mainly iron and nickel, that makes up the Earth's outer core. The inner core in the middle is solid, made up of iron and other metals.

Crust

Mantle

Continent

Ocean

Inner core

Outer core

Fire and ice

This bleak landscape in Iceland was created by the country's many volcanoes. Iceland is one of the most volcanically active places in the world and hardened lava covers most of the country.

Iron from space

Iron is also found in meteorites that fall to our planet from space. This 60-ton iron meteorite is the world's largest. It was found in 1920 at Hoba, Namibia, in south-west Africa. Scientists estimate that it fell to Earth less than 80,000 years ago.

A rocky layer cake

There are other rocks on Earth besides those made by volcanoes. Sedimentary rocks were formed out of sediment, or material produced when older surface rocks were worn away by wind and rain. These kinds of rocks build up in layers. This picture of the Grand Canyon in the USA shows an enormous area of sedimentary rocks. You can see how they are built up in layers of different shades.

ERUPTION

People usually think of volcanoes as mountains of fire that shoot fountains of red-hot rock high into the air and pour out rivers of lava. But much more comes out of volcanoes besides molten rock. Water that has been heated and turned into a gas in the volcano comes out as water vapour and steam. Once it is outside the volcano the vapour cools down and condenses (turns back into water). The hot rock inside volcanoes produces many other kinds of gas, such as carbon dioxide. Some of these gases go into the air outside the volcano and some are mixed with the lava that flows from it. The second project shows you how to make a volcano that gives out lava mixed with carbon dioxide. As you will see, the red floury lava from your volcano comes out frothing, full of bubbles of this gas. In a real volcano, it is the gas that is mixed with the lava that makes the volcano suddenly explode. The gas bubbles and swells inside the volcano and pushes out the mixture of lava and gas violently.

Hawaiian fire
The gigantic Hawaiian volcano Mauna Loa erupted in 1984, sending rivers of red-hot lava cascading down its slopes. The lava came dangerously close to the coastal town of Hilo. If the lava had reached Hilo, the town would have been set on fire.

WATER VAPOUR

You will need: heat-proof jug (pitcher), pan, oven gloves, plate.

Adult supervision recommended

1 Fill up the jug with water from the hot tap. Pour the water into the pan. Ask an adult to turn one of the rings on the hotplates or gas ring on the stove and place the pan on it.

2 Heat the water in the pan until it is boiling hard and steam is coming from it. Ask an adult to hold a plate upside-down above the pan with the oven gloves.

3 After a few seconds, turn off the stove and remove the plate from the heat. You will see that the plate is covered with drops of water. This water is water vapour (steam) that has cooled and turned back to liquid.

1 Make sure the jug is dry, or the mixture will stick to the sides. Empty the baking soda into the jug and add the flour. Thoroughly mix the two using the stirrer.

ERUPTION

You will need: jug (pitcher), baking soda, flour, stirring rod, funnel, plastic bottle, sand, seed tray (without holes), large plastic bin lid, vinegar, red food dye.

5 Pour the vinegar into the jug. Then add enough food dye to make the vinegar a rich red. It is best to use a clear vinegar such as white wine vinegar.

2 Place the funnel in the neck of the plastic bottle. Again, make sure that the funnel is perfectly dry first. Now pour in the mixture of soda and flour from the jug.

6 Place the funnel in the mouth of the plastic bottle and quickly pour in the red-tinted vinegar in the jug. Now remove the funnel from the bottle.

3 Empty sand into the tray until it is half-full. Fill the jug with water and pour it into the tray to make the sand sticky but not too wet. Mix together with the stirring rod.

4 Stand the bottle containing the flour and soda mixture in the middle of the plastic lid. Then start packing the wet sand around it. Make the sand into a cone shape.

7 The sandy volcano you have made will begin to erupt. The vinegar and soda mix to give off carbon dioxide. This makes the flour turn frothy and forces it out of the bottle as red lava.

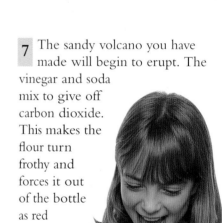

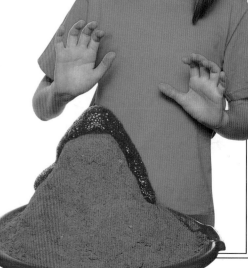

SPREADING SEAS

The Earth's crust is not all in one piece, but is made up of many sections, called plates. They are solid and float on currents circulating in the deep layer of semi-liquid rock beneath them in the mantle. All the plates of the crust move in different directions. Some plates are moving apart and others are moving towards one another. The plates that move apart are usually under the oceans. Magma pushes up from below the sea-floor and squeezes through gaps between the edges of the ocean plates. The magma squeezing up pushes the plates in opposite directions. As the plates move apart they make the ocean floor wider and push continents apart. This is known as sea-floor spreading. Sea-floor spreading builds up plates because when the magma cools it adds new rock at the edges of the plates. This kind of boundary between two plates is called a constructive boundary. The magma pushes up the seabed to form a long mountain range called a ridge or rise. Ridges are very noticeable features on the floors of both the Atlantic and the Pacific Oceans.

Underwater explorer
The deep-diving research submersible (midget submarine) *Alvin*. The submersible can carry a pilot and two scientific observers to a depth of 4,000m/13,000ft. *Alvin* can dive so deeply that scientists were able to study the Mid-Atlantic Ridge. The submersible also helped scientists to discover mineral deposits on the ocean floor.

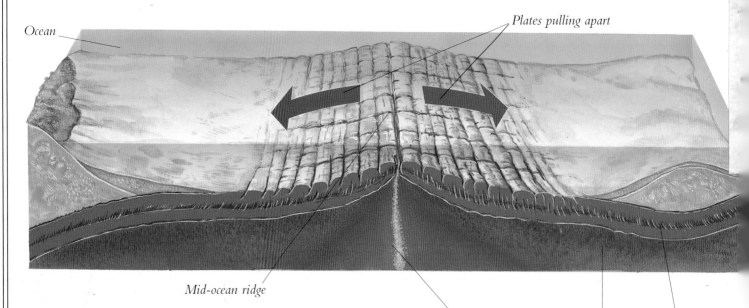

Ocean

Plates pulling apart

Mid-ocean ridge

Rising magma   Mantle   Plate

Along the mid-ocean ridge
A mid-ocean ridge forms when molten magma pushes its way upwards from the mantle, the semi-molten layer under the crust. The magma bubbles up through cracks in the crust as they are pushed apart. When the magma meets the sea water it hardens to form ridges.

Strange life

Hot water full of minerals streams out of the vents (openings) along the mid-ocean ridges. Strange creatures live around them. They include the giant tube worms pictured here around vents in the Galapagos Islands in the eastern Pacific Ocean. Other creatures that thrive on the ridges include species of blind crabs and shrimps.

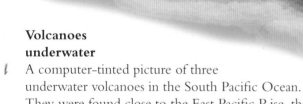

Volcanoes underwater

A computer-tinted picture of three underwater volcanoes in the South Pacific Ocean. They were found close to the East Pacific Rise, the main mid-ocean ridge in the Pacific Ocean.

New island

The island of Surtsey, off Iceland, did not exist before November 1963. In that month the top of an erupting volcano broke through the sea's surface close to Iceland. The volcano continued erupting for more than three years. There were times when the ash and steam rising from the new volcano reached more than 5km/3 miles into the sky.

Black smoker

Water as hot as 350°C/662°F, hotter than a domestic oven, pours out of vents along the ocean ridges. The water often contains particles of black sulphur minerals that make it look like smoke. This is why these vents are called black smokers.

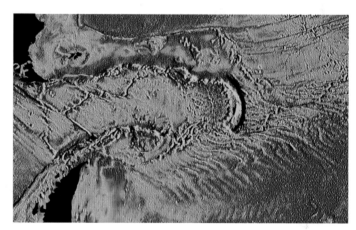

Plate and sandwich

A satellite view showing a small ocean plate on the floor of the South Atlantic Ocean between the tip of South America (top left) and Antarctica (bottom left). The curved shape in the middle is the South Sandwich Trench.

MOVING MAGMA

PLASTIC FLOW

You will need: lump of non-hardening clay, wooden board.

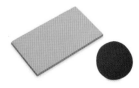

The temperature of the rocks in the Earth's mantle can be as high as 1,500°C/2,700°F. At this temperature the rocks would normally melt. They are under such pressure from the rocks above them that they cannot melt completely. They are, however, able to flow slowly. This is like a solid piece of clay that flows slightly when you put enough pressure on it. This kind of flow is called plastic flow. In places, the rocks in the upper part of the mantle do melt completely. This melted rock, called magma, collects in huge pockets called magma chambers. The magma rises because it is hotter and lighter than the semi-liquid rocks. Volcanoes form above magma chambers when the hot magma can rise to the surface. The second project demonstrates this principle using hot and cold water. The hot water rises through the cold because it is lighter.

1 Make sure that the table is protected by a sheet. Knead the lump of clay in your hands until it is quite flexible. Now shape it into a ball. Place it on the table.

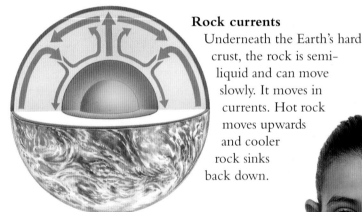

Rock currents
Underneath the Earth's hard crust, the rock is semi-liquid and can move slowly. It moves in currents. Hot rock moves upwards and cooler rock sinks back down.

3 Roll the clay into a ball again and press it with the board. But this time push the board forwards at the same time. The clay will again flow and allow the board to move forwards. The board is moving in the same way as the plates in the Earth's crust move.

2 Place the wooden board on top of the ball of clay and press down. The clay flattens and squeezes out at the sides. It is just like semi-liquid rock flowing under pressure.

1 Pour some of the food dye into the small jar. You may need to add more later to make your solution darker. This will make the last stage easier to see.

2 Fill the small jug with water from the hot tap. Pour it into the small jar. Fill it right to the brim, but not to overflowing. Wipe off any that spills down the sides.

3 Cut a circular patch from the clear film an inch or so bigger than the top of the small jar. Place it over the top and secure it with the elastic band.

BLACK SMOKERS

You will need: dark food dye, small jar (such as baby food jar), small jug (pitcher), clear film (plastic wrap), strong elastic band, sharpened pencil, large jar, oven gloves, large jug (pitcher).

4 With the sharp end of the pencil, carefully make two small holes in the clear film covering the top of the jar. If any water splashes out, wipe it off.

6 Watch what happens. The tinted hot water begins rising from the holes. This happens because the hot water is lighter, or less dense, than the cold water around it.

5 Use oven gloves to place the small jar inside the larger one. Fill the large jug with cold water and pour it into the large jar, not into the small one.

WHEN PLATES MEET

The plates on the sea floor that spread out from the mid-ocean ridges meet edge-to-edge with the plates carrying the continents. The edges of the plates then push against each other. Because continental rock is lighter than ocean-floor rock, the edge of the continental plate rides up over the edge of the ocean plate. The ocean plate is then forced back into the mantle inside the Earth. As the ocean plate goes down into the mantle, it melts and is gradually destroyed. This kind of boundary between colliding plates is called a destructive boundary because the edge of the ocean plate is destroyed. Where the ocean plate starts to descend, a deep trench forms in the sea-bed. The continental plate is also affected by the ocean plate pushing against it. It wrinkles up and ranges of fold mountains are formed. The great mountain chains of North and South America – the Rockies and the Andes – were formed in this way. Earthquakes also occur at destructive boundaries. So do volcanoes, as parts of the destroyed ocean plate force their way through the weakened continental crust.

Around the Pacific

Most of the Pacific Ocean sits on one huge plate moving north-west. This rubs against other plates and creates a huge arc of volcanoes (shown in red) along the plate edges.

Continental crust wrinkles up

Ocean trench

Ocean

FACT BOX

• The Andes Mountains of South America were formed by the collision between the South American plate and the Nazca plate. With a length of nearly 9,000km/ 5,600 miles, they form the longest mountain range in the world.

• The deepest part of the world's oceans is Challenger Deep, which lies in the Marianas Trench in the North Pacific Ocean. The depth there is almost 11km/7 miles.

Ocean plate

Continental plate

Ocean plate descends

Along ocean trenches

In many places around the world, a plate moving away from an ocean ridge meets a plate carrying a continent. When this happens, the ocean plate (which is made up of heavier material) is forced down underneath the continental plate. This causes a deep trench to form where the plates meet.

Youngest and tallest

The Himalayas in southern Asia form the highest mountain range in the world. They include Mount Everest which, at 8,848m/29,141ft, is the Earth's highest single peak. The range began rising only about 50 million years ago. The plate carrying India collided with the Asia plate at that time. The Himalayas is one of the youngest mountain ranges on Earth. In the long history of the Earth, 50 million years is not a particularly long time.

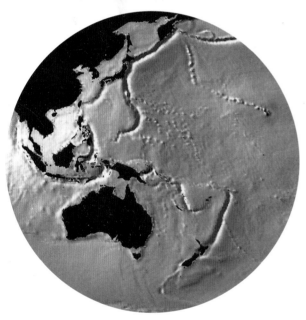

The ocean trenches

This satellite photograph of the Earth shows Australia at lower middle with the huge land mass of Asia at the top of the globe. The North and South Pacific Oceans are to the right, while the Indian Ocean is on the left. Variations in the height of the sea surface are clearly visible. The surface dips in places where there are deep trenches on the ocean bed many miles below. The deep trenches to the right of Australia in this view are the Kermadek and Tonga Trenches. The Marianas Trench is upper middle.

Volcanoes on the edge

The volcano on White Island, off the North Island of New Zealand lies close to an ocean trench, where the Pacific plate is descending. As the plate descends, it heats up and changes back to magma. This forces its way to the surface as a volcano. White Island volcano is one of hundreds that ring the Pacific Ocean. Together they form a ring of volcanoes which is called the Ring of Fire.

Above the clouds

The tops of volcanoes rise above the clouds on the Indonesian island of Java. Most of the country's islands lie near the edge of a descending plate and have active volcanoes.

HOT SPOTS

Most of the world's volcanoes lie at the edges of plates. A few volcanoes, however, such as those in Hawaii, are a long way from the plate edges. They lie over hot spots beneath the Earth's crust. A hot spot is an area on a plate where hot rock from the mantle bubbles up underneath. While the plate above moves, the hot spot stays in the same place in the mantle. The hot spot keeps burning through the plate to make a volcano in a new place. A string of dead volcanoes is left behind as the plate moves over the hot spot. Some form islands above the ocean surface. Others, called sea mounts, remain submerged. The best known active volcanoes far from plate boundaries are Kilauea and Mauna Loa on the main island of Hawaii. The Hawaiian archipelago lies in the middle of the Pacific plate, thousands of miles from plate boundaries. Its volcanoes erupt because it lies directly above a hot spot. The other Hawaiian islands formed over the same hot spot but were carried away by plate movement. In time, the main island will be carried away also. Volcanoes erupting from the hot spot will create a new island to take its place. The island of Réunion in the Indian Ocean is another example of a hot-spot location.

Powerful Pele
This is the name of the fire goddess of Hawaii. According to legend, Pele lives in a crater at the summit of the volcano Kilauea. When she wishes she melts the rocks and pours out flows of lava that destroy everything in their path. When Pele stamps her feet, the Earth trembles.

FACT BOX

• The Hawaiian hot-spot volcano of Mauna Kea is 9,000m/29,500ft high from the ocean floor. That is taller than Mount Everest. Half of Mauna Kea is below sea level.

• When sea mount volcanoes die, they cool and shrink. It is possible that the legendary lost city of Atlantis could have been built on top of a flat sea mount. Then the sea mount shrank and Atlantis sank beneath the waves.

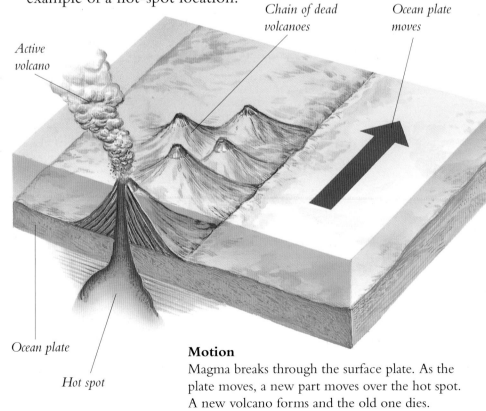

Chain of dead volcanoes

Ocean plate moves

Active volcano

Ocean plate

Hot spot

Motion
Magma breaks through the surface plate. As the plate moves, a new part moves over the hot spot. A new volcano forms and the old one dies.

Islands in line
Astronauts took this picture of the Hawaiian island chain in the North Pacific from the space shuttle *Discovery* in 1998. This island group is formed over a hot spot on the Pacific plate. The largest island is Hawaii which appears at the top of this picture.

Lanzarote's lunar landscape
Huge volcanic eruptions took place on Lanzarote, another Canary Island, in the 1800s and 1900s. They covered most of the island with lava and ash. The landscape is similar to the landscape on the Moon. Very few plants can grow in a landscape of this kind. Lanzarote has more than 300 volcanic craters. Many are to be seen in the area of the most recent lava flows, in the spectacular "Mountains of Fire".

Canary hot spot
Snow-capped Mount Teide, the highest peak on Tenerife, in the Canary Islands. It rises to 3,718m/12,200ft and was formed 10 million years ago by volcanic activity over the Canary Islands' hot spot. Teide last erupted in 1909.

Pacific atoll
There are many ring-shaped coral islands, or atolls, in the Pacific Ocean. These began as coral grew around the mouth of a volcano that rose above the ocean's surface. The the volcano sank, but the coral went on growing.

Pele is angry!
The volcano Kilauea, on Hawaii, is shown erupting here. At such times Hawaiians say that their fire goddess Pele is angry. She is supposed to live in Kilauea's crater. Kilauea, on the main island of Hawaii, is located over a hot spot on the Pacific plate. It formed only about 700,000 years ago.

CONES AND SHIELDS

Around the world there are more than 1,000 active volcanoes. They are all very different. Some erupt fairly quietly and send out rivers of molten lava that can travel for many miles. Others erupt with explosive violence, blowing out huge clouds of ash. The kind of magma inside a volcano makes the difference between it being quiet or explosive. Quiet volcanoes, such as those that form on the ocean ridges and over hot spots have magma with very little gas in it. The Hawaiian volcanoes formed over a hot spot. Their lava flows far, and they grow very broad. They are called shield volcanoes. Explosive volcanoes have magma inside them that is full of gas. Gas pressure can build up inside a volcano until it explodes. This is the kind of volcano found in the Ring of Fire around the Pacific plate. Because of their shape these volcanoes are called cone volcanoes. The blast and ash clouds these volcanoes give off can and do kill hundreds of people. The ash clouds can even cause changes in the weather. Large clouds of dust in the Earth's atmosphere from volcanoes block out the Sun's heat, making the weather on Earth colder.

Sticky rock
A volcano erupts with explosive force on Bali. It is one of a string of islands that make up Indonesia. There are more than 130 active volcanoes on the islands. They all pour out the sticky type of lava Hawaiians call aa.

Red river
A river of molten lava flows down the slopes of the volcano Kilauea on the main island of Hawaii. Like the other volcanoes on the island, Kilauea is a shield volcano. It pours out very runny lava that flows for long distances, usually at speeds up to about 100m/300ft an hour. The fastest lava flows are called by their Hawaiian name of pahoehoe.

Long mountain
The volcano Mauna Loa on the main island of Hawaii is 4,170m/13,000ft high. It is a shield-type volcano, meaning it is broad, with gently sloping sides. The main dome measures 120km/74 miles across and its lava flows stretch for more than 5,000 sq km/3,000 sq miles. In the Hawaiian language, the name means Long Mountain. This is a good name for it because it is very long and is the biggest mountain mass in the world.

Building layers

Explosive volcanoes blast rock and ash into the air. These eventually fall to the ground and lie there. Geologists call the rock and ash on the ground tephra. Here on Mount Teide, in Tenerife, layers of tephra have built up on top of each other after repeated eruptions.

Sacred mountain

Snow-covered Mount Fuji on the island of Honshu, Japan. Also called Fujiyama, it is one of the most beautiful volcanoes in the world and is considered sacred by the Japanese. It has an almost perfect cone shape. Five lakes ring the base of the volcano.

At the top

The caldera (crater) at the summit of the volcano Kilauea, on the island of Hawaii. There are vents (holes) in the caldera from which lava flows. The most active vent in the caldera is named Halemaumau. This is the legendary home of the fire goddess Pele.

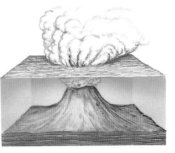

Submarine (undersea) volcanoes may grow in size until they rise above the surface of the sea. Scientists believe that this is how atolls are formed.

Hawaiian volcanoes have runny lava and gentle slopes.

Strombolian volcanoes spit out lava bombs in small explosions.

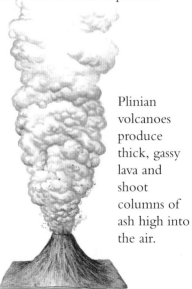

Plinian volcanoes produce thick, gassy lava and shoot columns of ash high into the air.

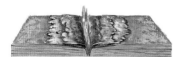

Fissure volcanoes are giant cracks in the ground from which lava flows.

Vulcanian volcanoes produce thick, sticky lava and erupt with violent explosions.

Pelean volcanoes produce clouds of very hot ash and gases. These clouds are dense and roar or gush quickly downhill.

Volcano types

Although all volcanoes behave in different ways, we can group them into a number of different kinds. In fissure volcanoes, magma forces its way up through long cracks in the Earth's crust. Then it flows out on either side and cools to form broad plateaus. Other volcanoes grow in various shapes caused by how runny or thick their lava is. Some of these volcanoes are famous for their violent eruptions of thick clouds of ash and gas.

FLOWING LAVA

LAVA VISCOSITY

You will need: two paper plates, jug (pitcher) ,jar of liquid honey, pen, stopwatch, washing-up liquid or soap.

1 Mark a large circle on the plates by drawing around the edge of a saucer. Pour a tablespoon of honey from the jar into the middle of the circle. Start the stopwatch.

In some parts of the world, there are ancient lava flows that are hundreds of miles long. Long flows like these have come from fissures (cracks) in the crust, which have poured out runny lava. Runny lava is much thinner than the lava produced by explosive volcanoes, which is sometimes called pasty lava. The correct name for the thickness of a liquid is viscosity. Thin liquids have a low viscosity, thick liquids a high viscosity. The first project below investigates the different viscosities of two liquids and how differently they flow. The second project looks at at the effect on substances of temperature. Heating solids to a sufficiently high temperature makes them first turn soft, then melt and then flow. Rock is no exception to this rule. If you make rock hot enough it softens, becomes liquid, and then flows. Deep inside a volcano, hot rock becomes liquid and flows up and out onto the surface as lava. When the lava comes out, its temperature can be as high as 1,200°C/2,200°F. This is the temperature of most of the runny lavas of the Hawaiian shield volcanoes. There are two kinds of lava flows from these volcanoes. One is called pahoehoe and the other aa by the Hawaiians. Volcanologists use these names for similar flows the world over. Pahoehoe and aa flows have different kinds of surfaces. Pahoehoe has quite a smooth skin and wrinkles up like coils of rope. Aa flows have a very much rougher surface that is full of rubble.

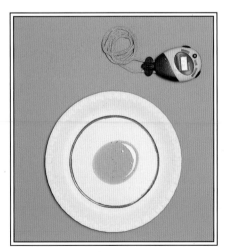

2 After 30 seconds, mark with the pen how far the honey has run. After another 30 seconds mark again. Stop the watch when the honey has reached the circle.

3 Part-fill the jug with washing-up liquid and pour some into the middle of another plate. Use the same amount as the honey you poured. Start the stopwatch.

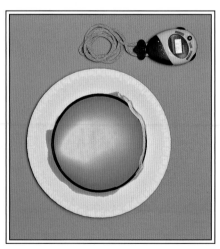

4 After 30 seconds, note how far the liquid has run. You will probably find that it has reached the circle. It flows faster because it has a much lower viscosity than honey.

MAGMA TEMPERATURE

You will need: block or a stick of margarine, jam jar, jug (pitcher), large mixing bowl, stopwatch.

1 Scoop out some margarine and drop it onto the bottom of the jar. For the best results, use hard cooking margarine, not a soft margarine spread.

2 Pick up the jar and tilt it slightly. See what happens to the margarine. The answer is, not a lot. It sticks to the bottom of the jar and does not slide down.

3 Fill the jug with hot water and pour some into the bowl. Shake it around to heat the bowl, then pour it away. Now pour the rest of the hot water into the bowl.

4 Pick up the jar and tilt it again. The margarine still will not move. Now place the jar on the bottom of the bowl. Keep your fingers clear of the hot water.

6 Continue checking the jar for another three or four minutes. After even a minute, the margarine will start to slide along the bottom as it warms and starts to melt. After several minutes, it is quite fluid.

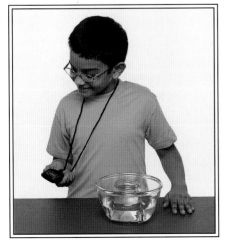

5 Start the stopwatch and after one minute, take out the jar. Tilt it, and see if the margarine moves. Return it to the bowl and after another minute, look at it again.

VICIOUS VOLCANOES

Erupting volcanoes can be among the most impressive sights in nature. They are almost always destructive, however, and can be deadly. Quiet volcanoes are the least dangerous to life, but their lava flows will destroy anything in their path. Explosive volcanoes are the most destructive. Their lava does not flow far because it is so thick. However, the clouds of ash, shattered rock and gas they blast out can be deadly. In AD79, exceptionally heavy ash falls from Mount Vesuvius covered the ancient city of Pompeii. When the volcanoes explode first, they often give off a glowing cloud of white-hot ash, gas, and rocky debris. This is called a *nuée ardente* (glowing avalanche) and can travel at speeds of up to 100kph/60mph. Such a cloud killed tens of thousands in St Pierre in the Caribbean in 1902. The gases that all volcanoes give out can also be deadly. They include sulphur dioxide and hydrogen sulphide. Both gases are highly poisonous. Vast amounts of carbon dioxide are also given off. This is not poisonous in itself, but it can kill by suffocation (inability to breathe). The carbon dioxide blocks out oxygen. When there is no oxygen, people cannot breathe. In 1986, more than 1,500 people and many animals died in this way at Lake Nyos in Cameroon.

Menace on Montserrat
Ash clouds billow high into the sky from this volcano in the Soufrière Hills on the Caribbean island of Montserrat early in 1997. Many people had to flee from the island.

Long ago in Herculaneum
The excavated remains of one of the houses in the Roman town of Herculaneum, near Naples in Italy. It was destroyed at the same time as nearby Pompeii in August AD79. It was blasted by hot gas and buried by repeated avalanches of hot ash and rock from Vesuvius.

Plaster casts of bodies

The Garden of Fugitives
In this part of the excavated city of Pompeii plaster casts of victims of the AD79 eruption of Vesuvius are displayed. Their life-like casts show how they huddled together in fear.

The death of Pompeii

On 24 August AD79, Mount Vesuvius, near Naples in Italy, erupted with explosive violence. A huge, choking cloud of gas, hot ash, and cinders blew down and covered the Roman town of Pompeii. At least 2,000 people are thought to have been killed either in their homes, or trying to flee from the deadly cloud. In a short time most of the city was buried. Over the past century more than half of the city has been uncovered. The ash and cinders have been dug away from many different buried buildings.

Silent killer

Carbon dioxide killed these cattle in fields near Lake Nyos, in Cameroon. The gas was released during a volcanic explosion under the lake in August 1986.

Lava rain

Volcanic bombs on the slopes of Mount Teide, on Tenerife, in the Canary Islands. They were thrown out during an eruption of the volcano as lumps of partly molten lava.

Gas sampling

A volcanologist takes a sample of gases from a volcanic vent. He wears a gas mask to avoid being suffocated.

Indian burial

The cinder field around Sunset Crater in Arizona, USA. The volcano that created the crater erupted in about AD1085. Thick lava flows, fumaroles (gas vents) and ice caves have been found in the surrounding area. It has been a US national park since 1930.

FACT BOX

• In April 1815 on the island of Sumbawa, in Indonesia, the volcano Tambora exploded. An estimated 90,000 people died directly from the eruption or from famine caused by ruined crops.

• In May 1902, a glowing cloud of gas from the Mount Pelée volcano on the Caribbean island of Martinique destroyed the city of St Pierre and killed its 30,000 inhabitants.

DANGEROUS GASES

The two projects here look at two effects the gases given out by volcanoes can have. In the first project you will see how the build up of gas pressure can blow up a balloon. If you have put enough gas-making mixture in the bottle, the balloon may explode. Be careful. When the gas pressure builds up inside a volcano, an enormous explosion takes place, often releasing a deadly hot gas cloud like the one that killed thousands of people in Pompeii. The second project shows the effect of carbon dioxide, a gas often given out by volcanoes. The project uses the gas to prevent oxygen reaching a candle. The candle cannot burn without oxygen. This explains how carbon dioxide kills people by suffocation: it stops oxygen getting into their lungs. The project also shows that carbon dioxide is heavier than air. Being heavy makes it dangerous because clouds of the gas can push away the air from around people and animals.

GAS PRESSURE

You will need: funnel, drinks bottle, baking soda, vinegar, jug (pitcher), balloon.

Plaster casts
Gas killed many of those who died at Pompeii. Archaeologists (people who study the past) can recreate the shapes of their bodies. First they fill hollows left by the bodies with wet plaster of Paris and let it harden. Then they remove the cast from the rock in which the bodies fell.

1 Make sure the funnel is dry first. Place it in the top of the bottle and pour in some baking soda. Now pour the vinegar into the funnel from the jug and into the bottle.

2 Remove the funnel. Quickly fit the neck of the balloon over the top of the bottle. Notice that the vinegar and soda are fizzing and giving off bubbles of gas.

3 The balloon starts to blow up because of the pressure, or force, of the gas in the bottle. The more gas given out, the more the balloon fills. Don't burst the balloon!

SUFFOCATING GAS

You will need: funnel, bottle, baking soda, vinegar, jug (pitcher), non-hardening clay, pencil, long straw, tall and short candles, large jar, matches and an adult to light the matches.

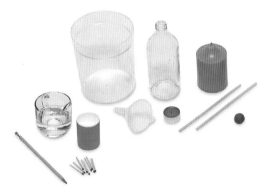

1 Place the funnel in the bottle and add the baking soda. Pour in the vinegar from the jug. This bottle is your gas generator. The gas produced is carbon dioxide.

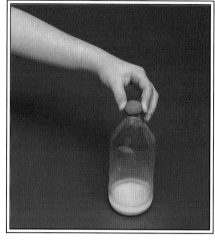

2 Knead a piece of clay until it is soft, then push it into the mouth of the bottle. Make sure it fits tightly. This will make sure that no gas will escape past it.

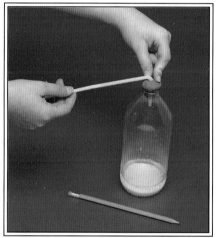

Deadly fumes
Clouds of poisonous sulphur fumes billow out from holes on the slopes of Mount Etna, on the Italian island of Sicily. It is one of the most active volcanoes in the world.

3 Make a hole in the clay stopper with the pencil. Carefully push the straw through the hole. Press the clay around the straw.

5 Direct the straw of your gas generator into the bottom of the jar. Keep your arms well away from the candle flames. Soon you will find that the short candle goes out. The carbon dioxide gas has covered it and blocked out the oxygen that would let it burn.

4 Stand both candles in the bottom of the large jar. Ask an adult to light them. Light the short one first to avoid the danger of being burned if the tall candle were lit first.

MOUNT ST HELENS

Picture perfect
Mount St Helens before the May 1980 eruption.

Mount St Helens lies in the Cascade range of mountains near the north-west coast of the USA. This mountain range includes many volcanoes. Before 1980, Mount St Helens had not erupted for 130 years. The mountain began to shake in March 1980. Scientists knew there was about to be an eruption. Many scientists and tourists came to photograph what would happen. The progress of the eruption was recorded by hosts of people on the ground, in the air and also by satellite. Nothing prepared the geologists who had gathered there, for the spectacular explosion on the morning of 18 May 1980, however. The blast, the ash clouds, the rain of debris from the volcano, the mud slides, and the poisonous fumes killed 57 people that morning. When the clouds cleared, the mountain had lost 430m/1,300ft in height and acquired a crater 3km/2 miles across. Mount St Helens was no longer a beautiful piece of tourist scenery.

Blast off
An enormous cloud of thick ash billows from the huge new crater formed when the top of Mount St Helens blew off on 18 May 1980. The cloud rose to a height of more than 20km/12 miles. It dropped ash over the surrounding region and on towns far away as it blew towards them. In some towns the ash blocked out the Sun. The city of Yakima was particularly badly hit. Over 500,000 tons of ash later had to be removed from the area surrounding Mount St Helens.

Before and after
These satellite photographs of the Mount St Helens region were taken before and after the eruption. They show how much land was devastated and covered by ash. The picture on the left was taken a few months before the eruption occurred. The mountain's snow cap is beginning to grow as autumn sets in. The picture on the right was taken about a year later. Ash covers thousands of hectares/acres of what was once forest land.

Like ninepins

This photograph shows what remained of a forest on the slopes of Mount St Helens after it erupted. Thousands of trees were knocked over by the powerful blast. In places the fallen trees were swept away by an avalanche of rocks, dust and mud, which caused even greater destruction.

Ominous dome

Since the 1980 eruption, Mount St Helens has been quiet. Domes like this near the summit show that magma is still pushing up to the top of the volcano, however. This shows that it is still active.

FACT BOX

• Native Americans of the Pacific Northwest called Mount St Helens *Tah-one-lat-clah* (fire mountain).

• Mount St Helens was previously active between 1832 and 1857.

• The first indication of a forthcoming eruption occurred on 20 March 1980, when an earthquake measuring over 4 on the Richter scale was recorded in the Mount St Helens area.

• On 27 March an explosion rocked the area, caused by an eruption of steam.

• Mount St Helens blew up at precisely 8.32 on the morning of 18 May 1980.

• The crater formed by the eruption measured 3.8km/2 miles long and 1.9km/1 mile wide.

Dark as night

Seven hours after Mount St Helens blew, street lighting was needed 140km/ 85 miles away in the town of Yakima because the air was filled choking dust.

Blooming again

Only a year after the eruption in 1980, plants are making a comeback on Mount St Helens. Flowers are blooming again on slopes washed clean by rain, and shrubs are pushing their way through the ash.

VOLCANIC ROCKS

The lava that flows out of volcanoes eventually cools, hardens and becomes solid rock. Volcanoes can give off several different kinds of lava that form different kinds of rocks. All these rocks are known as igneous, or fire-formed rocks, because they were born in the fiery heart of volcanoes. They contrast with sedimentary rock, the other main kind of rock found in the Earth's crust. This was formed from layers of silt that built up in ancient rivers and seas. Two of the main kinds of igneous rocks formed by volcanoes are basalt and andesite. Basalt is the rock most often formed from runny lava. This kind of lava pours out of the volcanoes on the ocean ridges and over hot spots. It is dark and dense. Andesite is the rock most often formed from the pasty lava that comes out of the explosive volcanoes on destructive plate boundaries. Because the crystals in both rocks are very small, they are called fine-grained rocks.

Road block
Lava flowing from the Kilauea volcano on Hawaii has cut off one of the island's roads. When the flow stopped, the molten lava had solidified into black volcanic rock with a smooth surface.

Intrusions
Here in Lanzarote, in the Canary Islands, molten rock has intruded, or forced its way through, other rock layers and then hardened. When this happens, geologists call it an intrusion. Volcanic intrusions like this most often occur underground when molten rock forces its way towards the surface. Sheet-like intrusions are known as dykes if they are vertical. If intrusions are horizontal and form between the rock layers, or strata, geologists call them sills.

Obsidian

This volcanic rock is formed when lava cools very quickly. It looks like black glass and is often called volcanic glass.

Basalt

Dark, heavy basalt is one of the most common volcanic rocks. This sample is known as vesicular basalt because it is riddled with holes.

Andesite

Andesite is lighter in coloration than basalt. It is so-called because it is the typical rock found in the Andes Mountains.

Rhyolite

This is another fine-grained rock like basalt and andesite. It is much lighter in coloration and weight than the other two, however.

Pumice

Pumice is a very light rock that is full of holes. It forms when lava containing a lot of gas pours out of underwater volcanoes.

Tuff

Tuff is rock formed from the ash ejected in volcanic eruptions. It is fine-grained and quite soft and porous.

The wrinkly skin

The runny type of lava called pahoehoe quickly forms a skin on its surface. This cools first. The lava underneath is still moving and causes the skin to fold and wrinkle. In large flows the surface may cool to form a solid crust, while lava still runs underneath.

Ropy lava

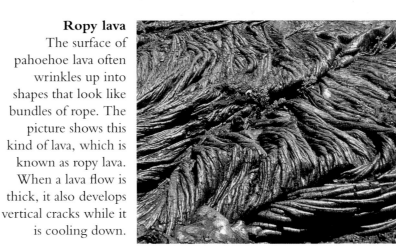

The surface of pahoehoe lava often wrinkles up into shapes that look like bundles of rope. The picture shows this kind of lava, which is known as ropy lava. When a lava flow is thick, it also develops vertical cracks while it is cooling down.

Sandy shores

In most parts of the world, the beaches are covered with pale yellow sand. But in volcanic regions, such as here in Costa Rica, the beaches have black sand. The sand has been formed by the action of the sea beating against dark volcanic rocks and grinding them into tiny particles.

BUBBLES AND INTRUSIONS

Rock slice
A highly magnified picture of a thin slice of the intrusive rock called andesite. When looked at through a microscope, it is possible to see the tiny crystals in this slice of rock.

In the first project on this page we see how keeping a liquid under pressure stops gas from escaping. The liquid magma in volcanoes usually has a lot of gas dissolved in it. As it rises through the volcano, the pressure drops and the gases start to leak. They help push the magma up and out if the vent is clear. But if the vent is blocked, the gas pressure builds up and eventually causes the volcano to explode. The lava that comes from volcanoes with gassy magma forms rock riddled with vesicles (holes). The pasty lava from some explosive volcanoes sometimes contains so much gas that it forms a light, frothy rock that floats on water. We know this rock as pumice. When rising magma becomes trapped underground, it forces its way into gaps in the rocks and between the rock layers. This process is known as intrusion. The rocks that form when the magma cools and solidifies are called intrusive rocks. Granite is the most common intrusive rock. Often the heat of the intruding magma changes the surrounding rocks. They turn into what are called metamorphic (changed form) rocks, and are the third main rock type, after igneous and sedimentary.

DISSOLVED GAS

You will need: small jar with tight-fitting lid, bowl, jug (pitcher), antacid tablets.

3 Now quickly unscrew the lid from the jar, and see what happens. The whole jar starts fizzing. Removing the lid releases the pressure, and the gas in the liquid bubbles out.

1 Stand the jar in the bowl. Pour cold water into the jar from the jug until it is nearly full to the top. Break up two antacid tablets and drop them into the jar.

2 Quickly screw the lid on the jar. Little bubbles will start to rise from the tablets but will soon stop. Pressure has built up in the jar and prevents any more gas escaping.

IGNEOUS INTRUSION

You will need: plastic jar, bradawl/awl (hole punch), pieces of broken tiles, non-hardening clay, tube of toothpaste.

1 Make a hole in the bottom of the plastic jar with a bradawl, enough to fit the neck of the toothpaste tube in. Keep your steadying hand away from the sharp end of the bradawl.

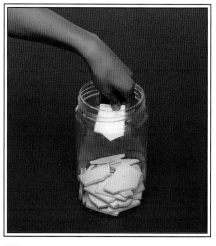

2 Place the pieces of broken tiles on the bottom of the jar. Keep them as flat as possible. They are meant to represent the layers of rocks we find in the Earth's crust.

3 Flatten out the clay into a circle that is as wide as the inside of the jar. Then place the circle of clay inside the jar. Push it down firmly on top of the tiles.

5 Squeeze the toothpaste tube. You will see the toothpaste pushing, or intruding, into the tile layers and making the circle on top rise. Molten magma often behaves in the same way. It intrudes into rock layers and makes the Earth's surface bulge.

4 Unscrew the top of the toothpaste tube. and force the neck into the hole you have made in the bottom of the bottle. You may have to widen it a little to get the neck in, but don't make it too wide.

FIERY MINERALS

Some of the rocks that volcanoes produce are very useful to people because they contain valuable minerals. These minerals are a source of metals, such as copper, silver and gold. Minerals are compounds (combinations) of chemical elements that are in the Earth. They form in the intense heat of volcanoes. Rock from volcanoes, such as basalt, looks as though it is a solid black lump. If you look at it under a microscope, however, you can see millions of little specks. These specks are crystals of minerals. The mineral crystals need time to grow. Lava cools so quickly that this does not happen. In volcanic rocks that cool more slowly, crystals have time to grow big enough to see without a microscope. Granite is a rock that forms when magma cools slowly underground. It contains three main kinds of mineral crystals: milky white quartz, pink feldspar, and black mica. Some of the most valuable mineral materials occur in streaks, or veins, in the rocks. They include ores (minerals from which metals such as the lead ore galena can be extracted) and precious metals such as gold.

Quartz crystals
Pure quartz is colourless and is known as rock crystal. It forms hexagonal (six-sided) crystals that end in pyramid shapes. Coloured crystals, such as amethyst, are used as precious stones.

A slice of olivine
The tiny crystals in olivine can be seen here in many different shades. Olivine is a mineral often found in volcanic rocks. A special kind of light called polarized light has been shone through a very thin slice of the olivine. Then the slice has been viewed through a special microscope. Transparent, pale green crystals of olivine, known as peridot, are used as gems in the making of jewellery.

Friend or foe?
Most volcanoes give off sulphur when they erupt, and this can collect into huge deposits after a time. Here a worker is cutting sulphur from deposits found around a volcano in Indonesia. Sulphur is very useful in modern industry but it can damage the lungs of those who mine it.

Bomb filling
Volcanic bombs such as these are often blasted out by erupting volcanoes. They are made of cooled lava and may contain other pieces of rock. Inside this bomb a chunk of peridotite was found. Peridotite is a volcanic rock tinged green by olivine crystals.

As nature intended
A diamond pictured in the rock in which it was found. When dug from the Earth, diamonds look rather like dirty glass. Only when they are expertly cut and polished do they display their outstanding beauty and sparkle.

For industry
This collection of diamonds has been cut and polished. They will not be turned into expensive jewels, however. Their shade is not pure enough and they contain flaws. They are industrial diamonds, which will be used, for example, in drill bits for cutting into rock. Diamond is the hardest of all the minerals on the Earth.

In the vein
The silvery crystals in this rock sample are of the mineral galena, which forms cubic crystals. It is one of the main ores of lead and often contains the metal silver. It is often found with zinc and silver minerals.

Beautiful beryl
Crystals of emerald, one of the finest gems, can be seen buried in a mass of quartz from Colombia, in Central America. Emerald is the green variety of a mineral called beryl. Other varieties of beryl are gemstones too, including aquamarine, a bluish-green mineral.

VOLCANIC LANDSCAPES

Blooms in a cinder desert
Hot cinders once blanketed the ground here. Since then wind-blown seeds have settled, germinated, grown into plants, and flowered. Their roots will help break down the cinders into better soil.

The landscapes in active or recently active volcanic regions are drab and bare and do not look as if they could ever be covered with vegetation. However, they are not without beauty, and in time, plants will grow there. The constant action of wind, rain, heat and frost eventually breaks down the newly-formed rocks. The rocks turn into soil, in which wind-blown seeds soon germinate. Providing the climate is suitable, flowers, shrubs, and finally trees will eventually grow again. Sprinklings of ash from further eruptions may, in time, add to and increase the fertility of the soil. But there is always the danger that when a volcano erupts it will destroy all the plants that have grown since the last eruption. This can happen in hours. After the enormous eruption of Mount St Helens in 1980, the blast, hot ash cloud and mud avalanches killed everything within 25km/15 miles. Less than a month afterwards, however, wildflowers began to grow, and soon insects and small animals began returning.

Dead landscape
A typical volcanic landscape in Iceland looks bleak before regeneration. Volcanic peaks tower in the distance, while in the foreground are bare, black volcanic rocks. Winter is coming, and temperatures are struggling to rise above freezing point. Conditions do not seem favourable for plant life.

Suitable soil
Here in another part of Iceland, the ground is carpeted with low-growing plants. They are growing in the thin soil that now covers a former lava field. The action of the weather and primitive plants such as mosses and lichens have broken down the lava into soil deep enough to support larger plants.

Etna's attractions

Giant cinder cones known as the Silvestri craters are on the southern side of Mount Etna in Sicily. The 3,330m/11,100ft-high mountain erupts frequently. It is one of a string of volcanoes in the Mediterranean region. The others include Stromboli, Vulcano and, most famously, Vesuvius. Geologists estimate that Mount Etna has probably been active for more than 2.5 million years. More than 110 eruptions of the volcano have been recorded since 1500BC. A particularly long eruption in 1992 destroyed much farmland and threatened several villages. The city of Catania, on the lower slopes of the mountain, is often showered with ash.

Rich paddies

Terraces of paddy fields are built on the slopes of hillsides in Bali in Indonesia, south-east Asia. The soil is very fertile because of the ash blasted out by the many volcanoes on the island. Terracing helps increase the amount of farming land and conserves water. In the hot, humid conditions, farmers can grow several crops of rice every year.

Fruit of the vine

Grape vines grow in vineyards on fertile land on the Italian island of Sicily. The land has been fertilized for centuries by the ash from regular eruptions of the island's famous volcano Mount Etna, which looms menacingly on the skyline. Etna is Europe's most active volcano.

Unstoppable

Nothing can stop this thick ribbon of lava, from an erupting volcano named Kimanura, smashing its way through tropical forest in Zaire. There are a number of active volcanoes along Zaire's eastern border. The border is in the Great Rift Valley, where plates meet, causing volcanic activity.

LETTING OFF STEAM

Hothouses
Here in Iceland, the greenhouses are heated by hot water piped in from the many hot springs in the rocks. The people of Iceland rely more on geothermal heating than any other nation.

The molten rock, or magma, in the earth's mantle does not always break out to create volcanoes. Sometimes it stays beneath the Earth's crust. There it causes other volcanic features. They are called geothermal features because they are almost always caused by the Earth (geo) creating heat (thermal) in underground magma that then affects underground water. The most spectacular geothermal feature is the geyser. This is a fountain of steam and water that erupts from holes in the ground. Vents (holes) called fumaroles, where steam escapes gently, are more common. They may also give out carbon dioxide and sulphurous fumes. Also common are hot springs, where water becomes heated in underground rocks to a temperature above body heat (about 37°C/98.7°F). Some hot springs can be twice this hot. Many are rich in minerals. For centuries people have believed that bathing in these mineral-rich springs is good for health.

Iceland *geysir*
A column of steam and water spurts out of the ground and high into the air as Iceland's Strokkur geyser erupts. It is just one of hundreds of geysers found in Iceland. The word geyser comes from the Icelandic word *geysir* (upwards force). Geysers may erupt every few days or hours. Some erupt at such exactly regular intervals that people can set their watches by them.

Boiling tar
In a volcanically active region in New Zealand, geothermal heating is causing this tarpit to boil and bubble. New Zealand was one of the first countries to tap geothermal energy for power production.

Hot dip

Icelanders enjoy the pleasures of a hot spring. There are hundreds of hot springs dotted around the island. The water from some of them is piped into towns to provide a cheap form of central heating for public buildings and homes. Geothermal heating has many advantages over conventional systems. It does not cause any pollution and will be available until the Earth cools in billions of years from now.

Yellowstone springs

A hot spring makes an impressive sight in Yellowstone National Park in Wyoming, USA. The intense blue of the clear water contrasts with the yellow and orange minerals that have been deposited by evaporation around the edges. Yellowstone is the foremost geothermal region in the USA.

Gleaming terraces

Looking like a frozen waterfall, white terraces of travertine are found in many hot-spring regions, as here in Yellowstone National Park, USA. Travertine is made up of the mineral calcite.

Steam power

A geothermal power station in Iceland makes use of natural geyser activity. Steam is piped up from underground and fed to turbogenerators to produce electricity.

FACT BOX

• One of the most famous geysers in the world is Old Faithful, in Yellowstone National Park in Wyoming, USA. This geyser erupts regularly about once every 90 minutes.

• Yellowstone National Park also boasts the tallest geyser in the world. Known as Steamboat, its spouting column has been known to reach a height of more than 115m/375ft.

GEYSERS AND MUDLARKS

All the different kinds of thermal (heat) activity that go on in volcanic regions have the same basic cause. Water on the Earth's surface trickles down through holes and cracks into underground rocks that have been heated by hot magma far below. The water becomes superheated to temperatures far above boiling point (100°C/355°F). It does not boil, however, because it is under huge pressure. Eventually, this very hot water may turn to steam and escape from a fumarole (vent where steam escapes). The hot water can also mix with cooler water to create a hot spring, or with mud to form a bubbling mud hole. Sometimes it turns into steam at the bottom of a column of water, creating a steam explosion that blasts water out of the ground as a geyser. The first project shows you how to make a geyser using air pressure to force out water. Blowing into the top of the bottle increases the air pressure there. This forces the water out of the bottle through the long straw.

Waterspout
Superheated steam and water spout high into the air from the Lady Knox geyser at Waiotapu, in New Zealand. A cone of minerals has built up around the mouth of the geyser, which usually erupts for about an hour.

GEYSER ERUPTION

You will need: non-hardening clay, long bendy straws, jug (pitcher), food dye, large plastic bottle, large jar.

3 Place the jar under the other end of the lengthened straw and blow into the other straw. Water spurts out into the jar. If the long straw was upright, the water would spout upward like a geyser.

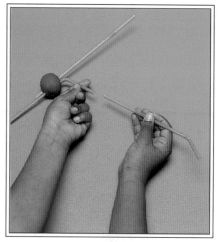

1 Make two holes in a little ball of clay and push two bendy straws through it as shown in the picture. Push another straw through the end of one of the first two straws.

2 Pour water into the jug and add the food dye. Then pour it into the bottle. Push the clay stopper into the neck so that the lengthened straw dips into the water.

MUDBATHS

You will need: cornflour (cornstarch), chocolate powder, measuring jug (pitcher), bowl, wooden spoon, milk, pan, oven glove.

Adult supervision recommended

1 Mix together two tablespoons of cornflour and two of chocolate powder in the bowl, using the spoon. Stir the mixture thoroughly until evenly mixed.

2 Pour about 300ml/1¼ cups of milk into the pan. Ask an adult to heat it slowly on the stove. Keep the heat low to make sure the milk does not boil. Do not leave unattended.

3 Add some cold milk, little by little, to the mixture of cornflour and chocolate in the bowl. Stir vigorously until the mixture has become a thick smooth cream.

4 Pour the creamy mixture into the hot milk in the pan, still keeping the stove on a low heat. Holding the handle of the pan with the oven glove, stir constantly to prevent the thick liquid sticking to the bottom of the pan.

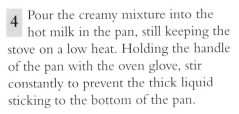

6 Soon your hot liquid mud will start sending up thick bubbles, which will burst with gentle plopping sounds. This is exactly what happens in hot mud pools in volcanic areas.

5 If you have prepared your flour and chocolate mixture well, you will now have a smooth hot liquid looking something like liquid mud.

CHANGING CLIMATES

Volcanoes can have a noticeable effect on the weather locally (nearby) when they erupt. Over weeks or months, they can affect climates around the world. Locally, volcanoes can set off lightning flashes. These break out when static electricity builds up in the volcano's billowing ash clouds and then discharges like a gigantic electric spark. The ash clouds from volcanoes may be so thick that they block out the sunlight and turn day into night. This happened for hours in the region around Mount St Helens after the eruption in 1980. It also happened for days during the eruption of Mount Pinatubo in the Philippines in 1991. The Mount Pinatubo eruption also had longer-term effects. The gas and dust it gave out stayed in the atmosphere (air) for months, producing spectacular sunsets. So much escaped into the high atmosphere that it cut down the sunlight reaching the ground. This cooled down the Earth's climate enough to affect weather patterns for a number of years. The Mexican volcano El Chichon, which erupted in 1982, had the same effect. Its ash had a particularly high sulphur content. Chemicals containing sulphur are believed to block sunlight most.

Mighty blast
In August 1883, the volcano Krakatoa blasted itself apart. The ash clouds from the volcano rose high into the atmosphere, spreading out and moving in a band around the world.

A dying breed
The fossil skeleton of a pterosaur, a flying reptile that became extinct (died out) about 65 million years ago. It might have perished as a result of the Earth being plunged into darkness after planetwide volcanic eruptions.

Blowing its top
The crater at the top of the Mexican volcano El Chichon. Until April 1982 it had a jungle-covered conical summit. But on 4 April, this was blasted away in an explosion that drove ash high into the atmosphere.

Fissure eruptions

This series of volcanic cones follows a long fault in Iceland called the Skaftar fissure. Massive ash eruptions occurred along the fissure in 1783 and caused cold winters in Europe.

Chilly winters

The ash and gases from volcanoes can stay in the atmosphere for years. If enough volcanoes erupted at the same time, winters could be much colder than usual. In very cold winters in the 1800s, people held markets called frost fairs on deep-frozen rivers.

Red night delights

Spectacular sunsets often occur when eruptions throw dust and ash into the air. In 1991, before Australians saw sunsets like this following the eruption of Mount Pinatubo in the Philippines. Mud slides that followed the eruption killed more than 400 people.

Ash cloud

The 2010 eruption of Eyjafjallajökull in Iceland created enormous disruption to air travel across western and northern Europe. Volcanic ash grounded thousands of flights and delayed hundreds of thousands of passengers, with flights to and from Europe being cancelled. It caused the highest level of air travel disruption since World War II.

FACT BOX

• The Indonesian volcano Tambora, which erupted in 1815, produced so much ash that world temperatures fell sharply in the following year. New England, in the eastern USA, had severe frosts in August.

• Mount Pinatubo, which erupted in the Philippines in June 1991, released nearly 8 cubic km/4 cubic miles of ash. This totals eight times as much ash as at the eruption of Mount St Helens.

OUT OF THIS WORLD

Earth is not the only place in the universe that has volcanic activity. Many other planets and moons in our Solar System have had volcanoes erupting on their surface at some time in their history. Two of the planets nearest to us, Venus and Mars, were affected by volcanoes. Venus and Mars are both terrestrial (Earth-like) planets, with a similar rocky structure to Earth. The whole landscape of Venus, revealed by the Magellan radar probe between 1990 and 1994, is volcanic. There are volcanoes everywhere. Most of the surface consists of vast lava plains stretching for thousands of kilometres. Mars has fewer volcanoes, but they are gigantic. The record-breaker is Olympus Mons, which is more than five times the height of Earth's highest mountain, Mount Everest. Nearer home, volcanoes have been a major force in shaping our Moon. The dark patches we see on the Moon at night are flat plains that flooded with lava when massive volcanic eruptions took place long ago. But some of the most interesting volcanoes lie much farther away, on one of Jupiter's moons, Io. Its volcanoes pour out liquid sulphur.

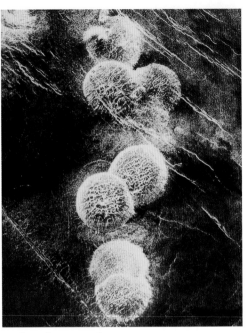

Volcanic pancakes
A series of volcanic features on Venus are called pancake domes. Scientists think they form when molten rock pours out of flat ground, spreads out and hardens.

The greatest
This is the biggest volcano on Mars, and one of the biggest we know in the whole Solar System. It is named Olympus Mons, or Mount Olympus. The volcano is 600km/370 miles across at the base, and it rises to a height of about 22km/14 miles.

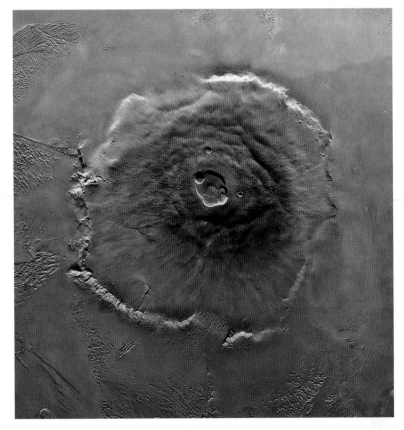

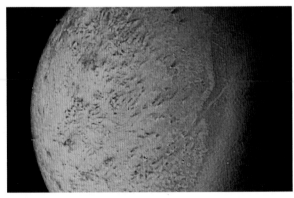

Triton's eruptions
Volcanic eruptions take place on Triton, the largest moon of Neptune. Because the moon is very cold (about −235°C/−455°F), its volcanoes give off liquid nitrogen. Dark material comes out as well, causing the dark streaks visible in the picture.

Out on a limb

A volcano erupts on the edge, or limb, of Jupiter's moon Io. It shoots gas and dust hundreds of miles into space as well as pouring molten material over Io's surface. The material that comes out of the volcano is not molten rock, however. It is a liquid form of the chemical sulphur. Sulphur is a yellow-orange, which explains why Io is such a vivid moon. Io's volcanoes were among the many astonishing discoveries made by the Voyager space probes. They visited the outer planets between 1979 and 1989.

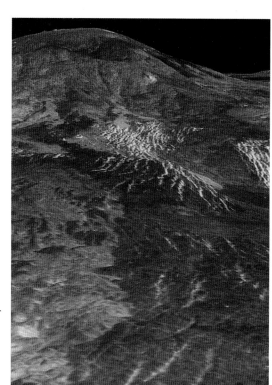

Volcano on Venus

One of Venus's many volcanoes recorded by the Magellan space probe. It has the typical broad dome shape of the shield volcanoes on Earth. Most volcanoes on Venus are of this type and, like all shield-type volcanoes, they pour out runny lava. Repeated eruptions over millions of years have sent rivers of lava streaming for hundreds of kilometres around. Most of the landscape of Venus consists of rolling plains made up of such lava flows. Venus's biggest volcanoes are up to 500km/300 miles across and several miles high, but most are much smaller. Venus has many other volcanic features, including strange, spidery structures called arachnoids.

The lunar seas

The seas on the Moon are flat plains. They were created billions of years ago when lava flooded into huge craters made by meteorites. The picture shows part of the Moon's largest sea, which is called the Ocean of Storms. This sea covers more than 5 million miles, and is more than half as big again as the Mediterranean Sea on Earth. The large crater in the picture is called Kepler by astronomers. It is about 35km/20 miles from one side to the other.

THE QUAKING EARTH

Famous fault
The most famous earthquake-producing fault in the world is the San Andreas in California, USA. It runs for hundreds of miles, passing close to the cities of Los Angeles and San Francisco.

Many people consider the city of San Francisco, in California, to be one of the most beautiful in the world. It has a stunning setting on the USA's west coast and enjoys a pleasant climate. But living in the city has one major disadvantage. San Francisco sits nearly on top of a line of weakness in the Earth's crust known as the San Andreas fault. The fault marks the boundary between two of the plates in the Earth's crust, the eastern Pacific and the North American plates. These plates are trying to slide past each other. They do this jerkily and when they do, the ground shakes violently. Earthquakes occur around the boundaries of all the plates on the Earth's surface, especially where the plates are colliding. This is why they often occur in the same places as volcanoes, which also occur at plate boundaries. Tens of thousands of earthquakes take place every year throughout the world, but only about 1,000 of them are powerful enough to cause damage. Such earthquakes are incredibly destructive. Most only last for a few seconds, but in that short time they can reduce whole cities to rubble and kill thousands of people. The main earthquake is always followed by smaller ones. These are called aftershocks and happen when the rocks along the edge of the fault settle into their new positions. These aftershocks can also cause a lot of damage.

Not so grand
This old print shows the chaos and destruction that earthquakes can bring. This earthquake was in 1843, in the port of Pointe-à-Pitre on the island of Grande Terre. It is one of the Guadeloupe group of islands in the Caribbean.

Housing slump
An earthquake in San Francisco in October 1989 caused whole rows of houses to collapse or damaged them beyond repair. In only a few seconds, more than 60 people were killed.

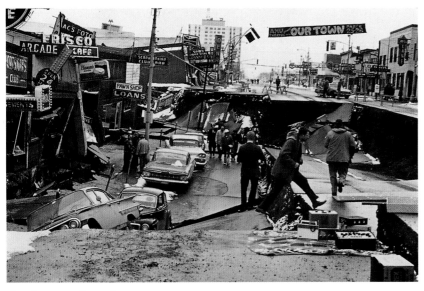

Anchorage in ruins
In March 1964, a powerful earthquake hit Anchorage, in Alaska. It was one of the longest ever recorded. The town and surrounding regions shook for four long minutes. Roads disappeared into the ground.

One-way street
An earthquake demolished one side of the Kalapana road in Hawaii in 1984. The ground was set shaking when the volcano Kilauea rumbled into life. Earthquakes occur frequently in volcanic regions.

No highway
In a 1994 earthquake that rocked Los Angeles, an elevated section of highway was shaken off its supporting piers (legs). Elevated roads are difficult to make earthquake-proof. The piers they stand on shake easily in earthquakes.

Kobe's killer waves
Some of the destruction caused by the powerful earthquake that struck the city of Kobe, Japan, in 1995. Multistorey apartment blocks collapsed like packs of cards. Japan has more earthquakes than almost any other country.

SLIPS AND FAULTS

Every earthquake, from the slightest tremor you can hardly feel, to the violent shaking that destroys buildings, has the same basic cause. Two blocks of rock grind past each other along a fault line where the Earth has fractured (the crust has split). There are several kinds of fault. At the San Andreas fault in California, the blocks are sliding past each other horizontally. This is called a transform fault, or strike-slip fault. In a normal fault, the rocks are pulling apart and one block slides down the other. In a thrust fault, the blocks are pressing together, causing one to ride up above the other. Because the edges of the blocks in contact at a fault are very uneven, friction (resistance to movement) locks them together. As they try to move, the rocks become strained and stretched. In the end, the strain in the rocks grows so great that it overcomes the friction. The two blocks suddenly move apart. The energy in the rocks is released as earthquake waves that cause great destruction.

All shook up
Traffic lights fell over in Los Angeles, USA, after an earthquake in January 1994 which killed 60 people.

FAULT MOVEMENTS

You will need: two wooden blocks, jar of baby oil, drawing pins (thumb tacks), sheets of sandpaper.

1 Hold a block in each hand so that the sides of the blocks are touching. Pushing gently, try to make the blocks slide past each other. You will find this quite easy.

2 Wet the sides of the blocks with the oil, and try to slide them again. You should find that it is easier. The oil has lessened the friction between the blocks.

3 Pin sheets of sandpaper on the sides of the blocks, and try to make them slide now. You will find it much more difficult. The sandpaper is rough and increases friction between the blocks.

QUAKES

You will need: scissors, strong elastic band, ruler, plastic seed tray (without holes), piece of cardboard, salt.

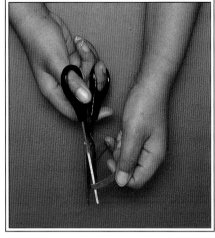

1 With the scissors, cut the elastic band at one end to make a long strip. This represents a layer of rock inside the Earth before it is affected by an earthquake.

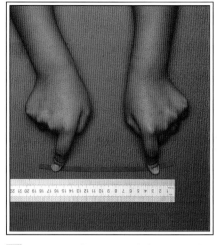

2 Measure the strip of elastic with a ruler. This represents the original length of the rock in the ground. Make a note of how long the elastic is at this stage.

3 Stretch the elastic band and hold it over the tray. Rocks get stretched by pulling forces inside the Earth during an earthquake.

4 Ask a friend to hold the card on top of the elastic and sprinkle some salt on it. The salt layer now on the card represents the surface of the ground above the stretched rock layer.

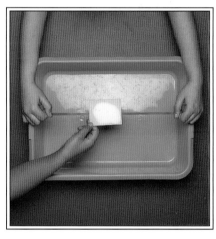

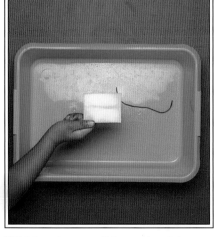

5 Now let go of the ends of the elastic. Notice how the salt grains on the card are thrown about. This was caused by the energy released when the elastic shrunk.

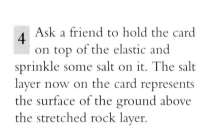

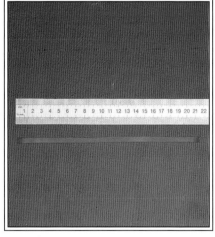

6 Finally, measure the strip of elastic again. You will find that it is slightly longer than it was at the start. Rocks are often permanently stretched a little after an earthquake.

No highway
Part of the elevated highway in Kobe that collapsed during the 1995 earthquake. The supporting columns were shaken into pieces by the force of the tremors.

TREMENDOUS TREMORS

The movement of rocks that causes earthquakes usually occurs deep inside the Earth's crust. The exact point where the rocks start to break, or fracture, is known as the focus. This can lie as deep as hundreds of miles or as close as a few tens of miles. At the surface, the most violent disturbance occurs at a point directly above the focus, called the epicentre. The closer the focus, the more destructive is the earthquake. The earthquake that struck Kobe, Japan, in 1995 was so destructive because its focus was only about 15km/9 miles deep. The focus of the great Alaskan earthquake of 1964 was not much deeper and caused massive destruction. The epicentre of that earthquake was on the coast of the Gulf of Alaska, and also caused the seabed to rise. This created a surge of water up to 21m/70ft high – it was a tidal wave, or tsunami. The tsunami devastated coastal towns and islands for hundreds of miles around.

Earthquake-proof
The Transamerica building in San Francisco is very distinctive. It has been built with flexible foundations. These should allow it to withstand the shaking that earthquakes bring.

Struts hold pipeline above ground

Flexible pipe
The Transalaska Pipeline snakes through the wilderness of Alaska, carrying oil south from the oilfields of the North Slope. It is built above ground. There are zigzags in places to allow it to move if and when earthquakes occur. The pipeline stretches for some 1,285km/800 miles.

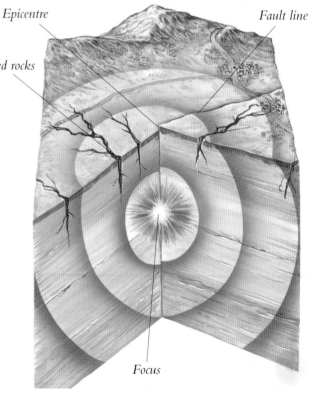

Epicentre

Fault line

Cracked rocks

Focus

Earthquakes in focus
Most earthquakes originate in rock layers many miles below the surface, at the focus. The most intense vibrations on the surface are felt immediately above the focus, at the epicentre.

Fire alarm

Fire breaks out in a gas main following a minor earthquake in Los Angeles. Underground pipelines carrying gas, oil or water are damaged easily when the ground vibrates. They can cause additional hazards to victims of the earthquake and their rescuers. The pipes break and their contents leak. Gas and oil catch fire easily. Water pipes can cause large floods.

Wall of water

This old print shows the tsunami (tidal wave) that followed the explosion of the volcano Krakatoa in 1883. Most of the people who died as a result of the eruption were drowned when this wall of water swept across the nearby low-lying islands.

Shipwrecked

One of the many fishing boats that were wrecked by the tidal wave that followed the powerful earthquake in Alaska in 1964. The wave devastated all the coastal communities around the Gulf of Alaska.

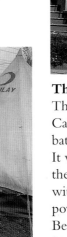

Displaced persons

Tents provide temporary shelter for the inhabitants of a town in nothern Turkey, following the earthquake in 1999. It was not safe to return home for weeks, even if houses suffered little damage. A main earthquake is always followed by a number of aftershocks. If these are strong enough, they may bring down even more buildings.

The safest?

This odd-shaped house in Berkeley, California, has four bedrooms, three bathrooms and was completed in 1995. It was specially designed to be one of the world's safest buildings by withstanding fires, floods and even powerful earthquakes – because Berkeley is not far from the notorious San Andreas fault zone.

MAKING WAVES

The enormous energy released by an earthquake travels through the ground in the form of waves. Some waves are rather like water waves. They can literally make the ground ripple up and down. Others make the ground shake from side to side, which makes them very destructive. Waves also travel deep underground from an earthquake. The primary (P) waves travel fastest. They travel through rocks in the same way that sound travels through the air, as a series of pressure surges (pushing motions). The secondary (S) waves are slower than the P waves. They travel up and down and from side to side. They are rather like the wave you can see in a rope when you shake it up and down.

Ripples in the street
The waves that travel through the surface rocks make the ground ripple. Afterwards, the ripples can often be seen. This road has been affected by waves in the ground. Now the surface of the road is like a wave.

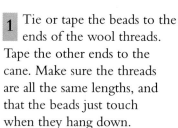

NEWTON'S CRADLE

You will need: large beads, lengths of wool (yarn), sticky tape, cane, four wooden blocks.

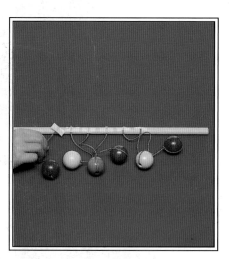

1 Tie or tape the beads to the ends of the wool threads. Tape the other ends to the cane. Make sure the threads are all the same lengths, and that the beads just touch when they hang down.

2 Prop up the cane at both ends on a pair of blocks supported by more blocks underneath. The blocks should be high enough to stop the beads from touching the table. Secure the ends with tape. Lift up the bead at one end of the row and let go. Look what happens to the other beads.

3 The beads in the middle do not move, but the one at the other end flies up. The energy of the falling bead at one end travels as a pressure wave through the middle ones. Then it reaches the bead at the other end and pushes it away.

TREMORS

You will need: set of dominoes, cardboard.

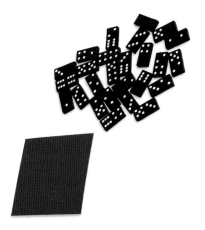

1 This project investigates how the energy in waves varies with distance. Near the end of a table, build a simple house out of dominoes. Stand them up on edge.

2 Place the card on the dominoes to make the roof of your house. Many people in earthquake zones live in the simplest of houses, built not too differently from this one.

3 Go to the opposite end of the table and hit it with your hand, but not too hard. What happens to your domino house? Probably it shakes, but still stays standing.

Leaning tower blocks
After a major earthquake, buildings lean at all angles as the shock waves destroy their foundations. The 1995 Kobe earthquake in Japan damaged nearly 200,000 buildings.

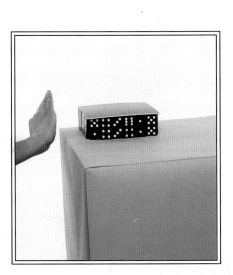

4 Now go back to the other end where your house is, and hit the table again with the same amount of force. What happens to your domino house this time?

5 Your house comes tumbling down. The waves you create when you hit the table are strong enough to knock down the house when it is nearby. When you hit the table from the opposite end, which is further away from the dominoes, the waves weaken as they travel. They are too weak to knock down the house by the time they reach it.

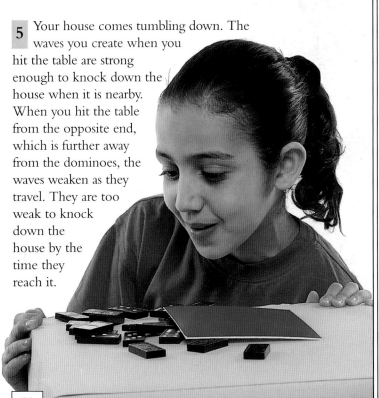

SEISMIC SCIENCE

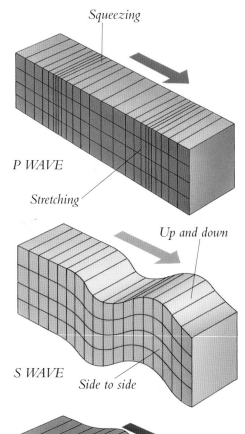

Squeezing

P WAVE

Stretching

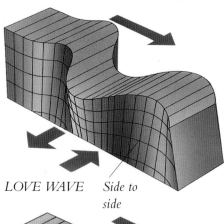

Up and down

S WAVE

Side to side

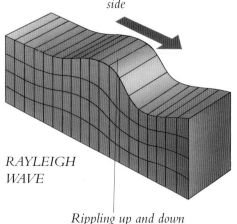

LOVE WAVE   Side to side

RAYLEIGH WAVE

Rippling up and down

Geologists who specialize in the study of earthquakes are called seismologists. These scientists call the waves that earthquakes create in the rocks seismic waves. The main instrument they use to detect and measure earthquakes is called a seismograph. Modern seismographs record the tremors (waves) an earthquake creates as a readout on a screen. The trace is known as a seismogram. It shows clearly the different waves earthquakes produce. The primary (P) waves, arrive first because they usually travel at speeds of more than 20,000kph/12,400mph. The secondary (S) waves arrive next. They usually travel at only about half the speed of the P waves. Finally come the surface waves. Among other things, seismologists can tell from a seismograph how strong an earthquake is. The strength, or magnitude, of an earthquake was measured on the Richter scale, invented by Charles Richter in the 1930s. In the new version, the MMS or Moment Magnitude Scale, the magnitude readings are very similar.

Making waves
This illustration shows four different ways in which earthquake waves travel through the ground. The primary (P) wave is a compression (squeezing) wave. It compresses, then stretches, rocks it passes through. The secondary (S) wave produces a side-to-side, shaking action. Love waves travel on the surface, making the ground move from side to side. Rayleigh waves are surface waves that move up and down. These two waves are named after the scientists who were the first to study them closely.

Charles Richter (1900-1985)
Charles F. Richter was a US seismologist. In 1931 he worked out a scale for measuring the relative strengths, or magnitudes, of earthquakes, based on the examination of seismograms.

On Vesuvius
An Italian seismologist looks at an old seismograph at the observatory on Mount Vesuvius, near Naples. The building dates from 1845.

Bad vibrations
This is a seismogram of a moderate earthquake in California, USA, in 1989. The widest vibrations show the strongest earth tremors.

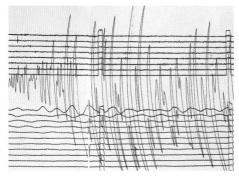

Looking for moonquakes

Apollo 11 astronaut Edwin Aldrin sets up instruments on the Moon in 1969. One was a seismometer, designed to measure moonquakes, or ground tremors on the Moon. Seismometers were set up at the other *Apollo* landing sites. They helped scientists work out the structure of the Moon.

Vibrating needle
A close-up picture shows the needle and drum of a seismograph. These machines have largely been replaced by electronic ones linked to GPS receivers and computers, able to record waves from earthquakes digitally.

FACT BOX

• The work in the early 1900s of an Eastern European meteorologist (weather scientist) named Andrija Mohorovicic led to the discovery of the layered structure of the Earth.

• The United States National Earthquake Information Center is one of the key seismic centres in the world. It records tens of thousands of seismic readings every month.

Electronic seismometer

A seismograph sits in the earthquake station under Aachen Cathedral in Germany. The geological service is monitoring the lower Rhine with 14 measuring stations. The area is one of the regions of central Europe with the highest risk of earthquakes.

BUILDING SEISMOGRAPHS

There are thousands of seismic centres scattered around the world. Within minutes of a quake, seismologists in different countries are analysing the seismograms from their seismographs. Then they will compare notes with scientists in other countries and will be able to pinpoint the epicentre and focus of the quake, its strength and how long it lasted. The Italian scientist Luigi Palmieri built the first seismograph in 1856. Older seismographs work on the same principle. They use a heavy weight supported by a spring inside a frame. When an earthquake occurs, it shakes the instrument. The heavy weight tends to stay where it is because of its inertia (resistance to change). A pen attached to the weight records the shaking movement as a wavy line drawn on paper wrapped round a rotating drum. The same principle of the inertia of a heavy weight is used to detect tremors in the do-it-yourself seismograph shown in the project here.

Out of a dragon's mouth
This is a model of a seismoscope built by a Chinese scientist of the past called Zhang Heng. The movement of an earthquake shakes a ball out of a dragon's mouth and into a toad's mouth below.

BUILDING A SEISMOGRAPH

You will need: cardboard box, bradawl (hole punch), sticky tape, non-hardening clay, pencil, felt-tip pen, string, piece of cardboard.

1 The cardboard box will become the frame of your seismograph. It needs to be made of quite stiff card. The open part of the box will be the front of your instrument.

2 Ask an adult to make a hole at top of the frame with the bradawl (hole punch). If the box feels flimsy, strengthen it by taping round the corners as shown in the picture.

3 Roll a piece of clay into a ball and make a hole in it with the pencil. Now push the felt-tip pen through the clay so that it extends a little way beyond the hole.

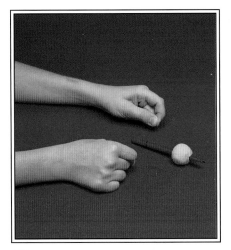

4 The pen and clay bob will be the pointer of your seismograph and make a record of earthquake vibrations. Tie one end of the piece of string to the top of the pen.

5 Thread the other end of the string through the hole in the top of the box. Now stand the box upright and pull the string through until the pen hangs free.

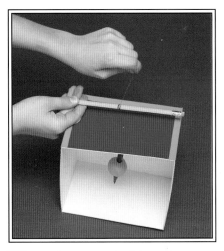

6 Tie the top end of the string to the pencil and roll the pencil to take up the slack. When the pen is at the right height (just touching the bottom) tape the pencil into position.

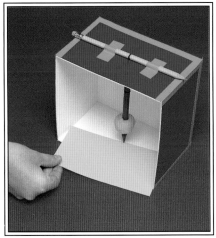

7 Place the card in the bottom of the box under the pen. If you have adjusted it properly the tip of the pen should just touch and mark the card.

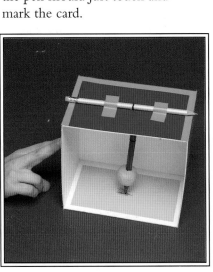

9 You do not have to wait for an earthquake to test your seismograph. Just shake or tilt the frame. The suspended pen does not move but it marks the piece of card, giving you your very own seismogram.

8 Your seismograph is now complete and ready for use. It uses the same principle as a proper seismograph. The heavy bob, or pendulum, will be less affected by shaking motions than the frame.

FIELDWORK

The scientists who study volcanoes and earthquakes spend a great deal of time in the field (on the spot) around active volcanoes and in earthquake zones (places where earthquakes commonly take place). Volcanologists keep an eye on many active volcanoes all the time, looking for any changes that may signal a new eruption. Permanent observatories have been built on volcanoes near centres of population, such as Mount Vesuvius and Mount Etna in Italy. Hopefully the volcanologists can give advance warnings to people who could be at risk. When eruptions do take place, they chart the direction of lava flows and take temperatures and samples of lava and gases. The thermometers they use are not the mercury-in-glass kind. Those would melt at 1,000°C/1,800°F and at the greater temperatures found around volcano sites. Volcanologists use thermocouples to measure temperatures. These are made of metals. Seismologists spend their time in earthquake regions setting up and checking instruments that can record ground movements. This is part of their study to try and predict earthquakes.

Studying creep
A scientist measures movements along a fault using a creepmeter. The two parts of the creepmeter are on either side of the fault line.

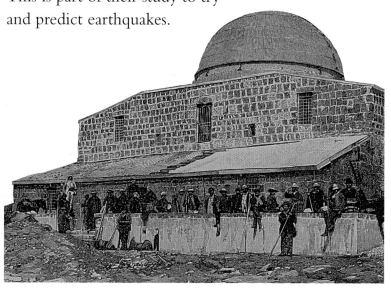

Watching Etna
Mount Etna, in Italy, is the highest volcano in Europe. It has been erupting for more than 2.5 million years. Shown above is one of the three observatories set up on its slopes in the mid 1800s. The town of Catania lies on the slopes of Mount Etna. The volcano is watched constantly because if it erupts it could destroy Catania and other villages nearby. Fortunately eruptions on Etna happen quite slowly.

Hard hat job
A geologist checks a lava flow from Hawaii's highly active volcano Kilauea. The sides have already cooled and solidified, which helps shield him from the heat given out by the river of molten rock beneath. He wears a hard hat to protect himself from falling debris.

Space age suits

These volcanologists look quite similar to astronauts in their protective suits. They are carrying out research in Ethiopia about the lava lake at Erta Ale volcano. The suits they wear have a shiny silvery coating. This reflects the heat from the hot lava away from their bodies and so helps to keep them cool. The researchers also wear protective helmets to shield their faces, particularly their eyes, from the heat. Erta Ale has been erupting since 1967.

Laser checking

Seismologists sometimes use a space satellite called Lageos to check for ground movements. Two identical lasers are set up, one on each side of a fault. Movement in the ground affects the time it takes for the laser beams to go to and from the satellite. These time differences tell the scientists the ground is moving.

On the ice

Geologists carry out seismic surveys in Antarctica to study the rock layers under the ice. In places the ice is more than 4,000m/ 13,000ft thick. Mount Erebus is the only volcano on the continent.

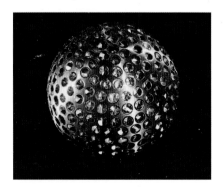

Lageos satellite

Thumping good idea

In the past, seismologists set off explosives to send shock waves they could measure through the rocks. Nowadays they mostly use special vibrator trucks, which thump the ground to create waves.

MEASURING MOVEMENTS

The seismograph is the most important instrument for seismologists once an earthquake has happened. But these scientists use many other instruments, in particular to detect how the ground moves in areas where earthquakes might occur. The San Andreas fault in California is criss-crossed with seismic ground stations, some using laser beams and other electronic devices and others with relatively simple instruments. An extensometer measures stretching movements in the rocks. A magnetometer detects minute changes in the Earth's magnetism that often occurs when rocks move. A creepmeter measures movements along faults. Our two projects show how to make simple versions of instruments called the gravimeter and the tiltmeter. The gravimeter measures slight changes in gravity. When changes occur, the pull on a heavy mass changes, which will make a mass and a pointer attached to it move over a scale. The tiltmeter detects whether rock layers are tilting by comparing the water levels in two connected containers.

Seismic survey
Seismic researchers carry out an accurate survey of the ground in an earthquake region. By comparing their readings with past records, they can tell if any ground movements have taken place.

GRAVIMETER

You will need: strip of sticky (contact) paper, pen, large jar, non-hardening clay, elastic (rubber) band, toothpick, pencil.

1 Draw a scale on a strip of sticky paper using a ruler and pen. Stick the scale on the jar. In a real instrument this would measure slight changes in gravity.

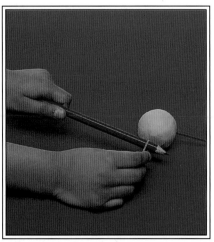

2 Bury one end of an elastic band in a ball of clay. Stick in a toothpick at right angles to the band to act as a pointer. Pass the pencil through the loop of the band.

3 Lower the ball into the jar, dangling from the pencil, so that the tip of the pointer is close to the scale. Rest the pencil on the top of the jar and use bits of clay to stop it moving. If you move the jar up or down, the pointer moves down and up the scale.

TILTMETER

You will need: bradawl (hole punch), two transparent plastic cups, transparent plastic tubing, non-hardening clay, pen, sticky paper, wooden board, adhesive, food dye, jug (pitcher).

1 Ask an adult to use the bradawl (hole punch) to make a hole in the sides of each plastic cup, just about half-way down. Be careful not to prick your fingers.

2 Push one end of the tubing into the hole in one of the cups. Seal it tight with clay. Put the other end in the hole in the other cup and seal this in the same way.

3 Using the pen, draw identical scales on two strips of the sticky paper. Use a ruler and mark regular spaces. Stick the scales at the same height on the side of the cups.

4 Stick the cups to the wooden baseboard with safe adhesive. Position them so that the tube between is pulled straight, but make sure it doesn't pull out.

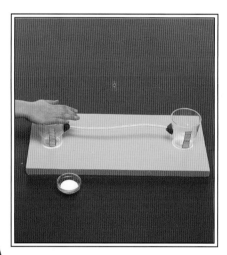

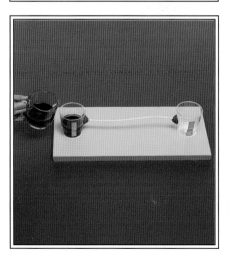

5 Add some food dye to water in the jug, and pour into each of the cups. Make sure to fill them so that the water level reaches over the openings to the tubes.

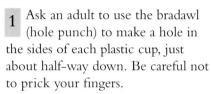
Tilt makes water flow out of upper cup

6 Your tiltmeter is now ready for use. When it is level, the water levels in the cups are the same. When it tilts, the water levels change as water runs through the tube from one cup to the other.

Tilt makes water flow down into lower cup

TO THE RESCUE

When volcanoes erupt and earthquakes strike, they can unleash destructive power equal to hundreds of atomic bombs. The most destructive volcanoes explode and cause ash and mud slides that sweep away everything in their path. Most people caught by these stand no chance and are dead by the time any rescuers can arrive. Earthquakes are even more deadly than volcanoes. They often kill thousands of people when their houses crumble about them in a few seconds. Many people survive the earthquake itself but are buried alive and often badly injured. It is then a fight against time to rescue them before they die of suffocation or their injuries. Many cities in earthquake zones have well-trained rescue teams. But when disaster strikes in remote villages it can be days before any teams can reach them. Often the roads to the villages have become impassable. All earthquake rescue work is hazardous. Aftershocks can bring down damaged buildings on the rescuers. Fire may break out from fractured gas pipes, and there may not be enough water for firefighting because of burst water mains. There can also be great danger of disease from the decaying bodies of possibly thousands of people and animals.

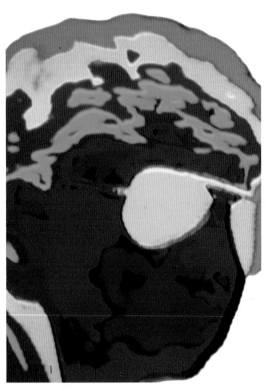

Body heat
This is a picture taken by a thermal imaging camera. It records heat, not light. Rescuers use these cameras when searching in dark places for earthquake survivors.

With bare hands
A survivor of the 1995 Kobe earthquake in Japan uses his bare hands to remove debris. He is searching for other members of his family who might be buried in the ruins.

Ash and mud
An aerial view of Plymouth, the capital of the Caribbean island of Montserrat, after the volcanic eruption of 1997. Thick ash and torrents of mud have covered the city.

Swept away
A Japanese man is found clinging to the roof of his house about 15km/9.3 miles off Fukushima prefecture, two days after a tsunami swept him out to sea. In March 2011, Japan was hit by a 9.0 magnitude earthquake, which triggered a deadly 7m/23ft tsunami. Giant waves destroyed cities and rural areas, sweeping away cars, homes and buildings.

Clearing up
Powerful excavators work round the clock to clear away shattered concrete and twisted metal supports from the collapsed Hanshin expressway after the Kobe earthquake in Japan. It took nearly a week to get the road back to normal.

Rescue man's best friend
Earthquake rescue teams not only rely on the latest scientific equipment to find survivors but also use sniffer dogs. Sniffer dogs are specially trained to use their sensitive noses to pick up the scent of people buried in collapsed buildings.

Trapped under rubble
Members of the Los Angeles County Fire Department Search and Rescue Team rescue a Haitian woman from a collapsed building following an earthquake in Haiti, January 2010. The woman had been trapped in the building for five days without food or water.

GLOSSARY

active volcano
A volcano that is erupting or might erupt at any time in the near future.

archipelago
A large group of islands.

atmosphere
The layer of air surrounding the Earth.

atoll
A small island made up of an almost circular strip of coral surrounding a lagoon of sea water.

climate
The typical weather pattern of a place over many years, even centuries.

constructive boundary
The edge of one of the Earth's plates, where new plate material is forming.

continental drift
The gradual movement of the continents across the face of the Earth.

core
The region at the heart of the Earth.

creepmeter
An instrument that measures movements of the Earth's crust along faults in the crust.

crust
The rocky surface layer of the Earth.

destructive boundary
A region of the Earth's crust where one of the plates of the crust is colliding with another and being destroyed.

dormant volcano
A volcano that is not active at present but might erupt one day in the future. The word dormant means sleeping.

earthquake
An often violent shaking of the Earth's crust, caused when plates in the crust try to slide past or over each other.

epicentre
The region on the Earth's surface that lies directly above the focus of an earthquake.

erosion
The gradual wearing away of the Earth's surface by the action of wind, rain, heat, cold, and the movement of rivers.

extensometer
An instrument that measures whether stretching movements are occurring in the rocks in the Earth's crust.

extinct volcano
A volcano that has not erupted for many years and is believed unlikely ever to erupt again.

fault
A crack in the Earth's crust.

focus
The exact point underground where the rocks in the Earth's crust move and cause an earthquake.

fossil
The remains in the Earth's rocks of living things that have died and been preserved.

fumarole
An opening in the ground in volcanic regions, where steam and gases escape.

geologist
A scientist who carries out the study of the Earth's surface and rocks.

geology
The scientific study of the Earth and the changes that take place on its surface and in the rocks below.

geothermal energy
The energy created in areas of volcanic activity by the heating of rocks below the Earth's surface.

geyser
A fountain of steam and water that spurts out of vents in the ground in volcanic regions.

gravimeter
An instrument that measures slight changes in gravity in the rocks in the Earth's crust.

hot spot
A place in the Earth's crust away from plate boundaries where hot rock forces its way to the surface to cause volcanoes.

hot springs
Places in volcanic regions where water that has been heated underground by rocks bubbles to the surface.

igneous rock
A rock that forms when magma (hot molten rock) cools and becomes solid. This can happen both on the Earth's surface or underground.

intrusive rock
A rock that forms underground when hot molten rock forces its way into existing rock layers and then cools.

lava
The molten rock that pours out of volcanoes onto the surface of the ground and then cools. Lava can be very thin and runny or thick and pasty.

magma
The name given to hot molten rock while it is still inside the Earth's crust.

mantle
The very deep layer of rock that lies underneath the Earth's crust.

metamorphic rock
Rock that forms when existing rocks are changed because of great heat and pressure inside the Earth's crust.

mineral
A chemical compound found inside the Earth.

nuée ardente
A glowing cloud of very hot air and ash given out by some volcanoes. It spreads quickly over the area surrounding the volcano, causing death and destruction on a large scale.

planet
One of the eight large bodies in the Solar System that circle around the Sun. The Earth is one of the eight planets.

plate
A section of the Earth's crust that moves in a recognised direction across the Earth's surface.

P waves
The primary waves produced by an earthquake that travel fastest and are detected first.

Richter scale
A scale for measuring the strength of earthquakes, devised by the US scientist Charles Richter.

sedimentary rock
Rock formed from layers of sediments, or materials such as eroded rock and chemical compounds that settled in layers millions of years ago at the bottom of seas and rivers.

seismogram
The wavy trace on paper or screen that a seismograph makes.

seismograph
An instrument used by scientists to record earthquake waves.

seismologist
A geologist who carries out the study of earthquake waves.

seismology
The study of the waves that earthquakes send out.

Solar System
The family of planets, moons and other bodies that orbit round the Sun.

S waves
The secondary waves produced by an earthquake, detected later than P waves.

thermocouple
A thermometer scientists use to measure very high temperatures.

thermometer
An instrument that is used for measuring temperature.

tidal wave
A tsunami or huge ocean wave caused when an earthquake takes place on the seabed. It has nothing to do with tides.

tiltmeter
An instrument used to detect the tilting of the ground.

tremor
A shaking of the ground.

trench
A valley in the seabed, marking the region where one plate of the Earth's crust meets another and is forced down into the crust.

tsunami
A huge ocean wave set up when an earthquake takes place on the seabed. It is popularly called a tidal wave.

vent
An opening in the ground.

viscosity
A measure of how thick or thin a liquid is. A liquid with low viscosity flows faster than one with a high viscosity.

volcanic bomb
A lump of molten material flung into the air from a volcano.

volcano
An opening in the Earth's crust from which molten rock escapes.

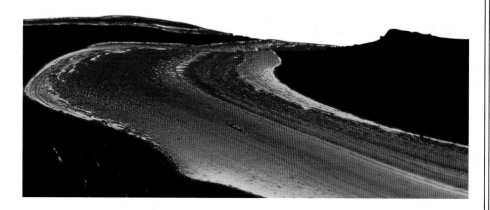

INDEX